A DIFFERENT JOURNEY

by Roy W. Taylor

First published   November 2016.

My thanks to Michelle McCabe for the cover design and to Elaine Amy McFeeters for checking the proof copy.

Amazon

Contents:

A Thai Prelude

It was a journey with a difference.

The short flight from Penang brought us to Hat Yai Airport, where we had to walk across the hot tarmac to the terminal building. At first we wondered why there were so many soldiers around. Surely our visit did not pose a great threat to the country! Soon we learned that this was because a 'plane was about to land bearing the King.

We were met by a taxi driver, who welcomed us into his vehicle. His wife joined us for the long ride to Saiburi. We spoke no Thai and she spoke no English, but she was set on making proper contact with us. So she would cradle her arms, making a rocking movement with them and then pointing at us. In return we raised two fingers. Point made!

Our destination, Saiburi, was a primarily Muslim area, where we were to attend a missionary conference. It was the sort of area where beachgoers had to cover their swimwear with more acceptable clothing such as a dress or shorts so as not to offend the locals.

Yes, it was a journey with a difference. Eileen and I were fortunate enough to enjoy many exciting journeys during our time together in many parts of the world, and much of the fun came from being together and thus sharing these experiences.

I still go on journeys, but now I go alone. When I mount the steps into the aircraft there is no companion and when I am seated there is either a stranger or a vacant seat beside me. Now I am on a different journey, as I once again lead the life of a single person. Can such a journey still be a positive experience? That is the question we shall examine here.

One.   Single Again.

A few years ago, after the death of my wife, I produced a book called "Lark Ascending", which I had felt impelled to write. Now, several years later, I sense it is time to write a sequel which looks at the next stage.

This is not a book full of examples about how well I have dealt with bereavement, but rather an honest account of what it has been like, together with a few suggestions and conclusions. If you also have suffered bereavement, your experience may have been very different from mine, but there will also be similarities, and I suggest that we can learn from one another.

(1) A Personal History.

First, however, let us go back into my personal history. At one time being alone was something that I actively sought. Way back in the 1960s I longed to get a place of my own. I had been through university and theological college. Now, in my curacies, as a single man, I had to board with others. In one parish it did not work out very successfully. In my second parish my landlady thought my main purpose in being there was to be a sort of companion to her. "You're not going out again, are you?" she would say. "You're never at home."

Two terms followed at a missionary training college, then I was off to Taiwan. After a short spell staying at the diocesan centre, I was able to rent a place. Just a small flat with two rooms and a small bathroom, but it had my name on it.

Two years later I moved to a job in the south of the country, and I found myself the sole inhabitant of a large Japanese bungalow with four bathrooms, once inhabited by an archdeacon and his family. The other building was a student hostel, but in the bungalow I was alone. I had got my wish – a place all to myself. But was that what I really wanted now? Was it not time to share it with someone special? What about those words from the Bible: "It is not good for man to be alone" (Genesis 2:18)?

I had had casual girl friends: this included the one in my home town who was desperately trying to get away from an unhappy family home, the likeable theological student who always seemed to have another boy friend, the pale skinned West Indian girl whose father was in the RAF, a missionary candidate who was called to Nigeria whilst I was called to Taiwan and an American missionary who had a real skill for accompanying her own singing on a guitar; but I did not feel that any of these was destined to become my life partner.

Then I met Eileen. It was not love at first sight. We got to know one another because we belonged to a little group of missionaries working in the same city who would meet up regularly for prayer and fellowship. Gradually I came to realize that there was something more about this particular relationship.

We began to go out together, and the relationship developed. A year after we first met, when we were both on furlough, we became engaged, and three months later, in the midst of Northern Ireland's 'troubles' we were married on a cold November day, followed by a honeymoon on the wintry north coast, but there was a warmth in our relationship which compensated for all that.

It was a joy to take Eileen back to share that bungalow with me. In due course our sons were born, and so we became a complete family. A few years later we returned to England, where I had successively a parish job, a travelling job and two further parish jobs. Over those years our love grew and grew.

It was so obvious to us both that it was the Lord who had brought us together and given us such fulfilment in one another and together in the Lord.

When Eileen had a sense that God was calling us to retire to a certain house by the sea in Northern Ireland I accepted the validity of that guidance, and we bought the property concerned, letting it out to tenants until we were able to move in ourselves on retirement in early 2003.

We looked forward to many happy years together. In those early years we did holiday chaplaincies in Spain and Tunisia, visited friends and relatives in the USA and in Australia and enjoyed sunshine holidays on various islands in the Mediterranean and the Canaries. It was while we were on holiday in Portugal that it became obvious that something was terribly wrong with Eileen's health.

Unknown to us at the time, we just had 11 months left together, and Eileen, because of her aggressive cancer, would be in no position to enjoy them. However, in a sense those months together were precious. I have described this period in detail in my former book.

(2) The Next Stage.

It is seven years at the time of writing since Eileen's death, and I feel the time has come to take a look at those years, to describe how I have felt and to indicate some lessons learned.

I am not writing as one who has all the answers. Although I have discovered some helpful tips, I am still learning. I do not pretend that I have always got everything right. For those who read what I have written, some sections may have nothing valuable to say, but others may hit the spot.

The other book was mainly a chronological account of our life together in those challenging months, and it also included extracts from the journal concerning our early days together. This book is arranged topically, but still draws heavily upon my experience.

I hope, however, to go beyond mere experience and consider issues which affect all of us who have been faced with bereavement or may face it in the future. I hope to examine how we may receive practical help from the Lord to deal with the emotions and the situations which concern us.

If we believe that a happy marriage is God-given, then we must also recognize that God is still with us when we have become single again. It is a challenging time. Even C. S. Lewis, according to his book, "A Grief Observed", found it an incredibly difficult period; but there is life beyond the sickbed and the graveside, and that is what we are going to explore together in this book.

It is my prayer that something here may strike a chord with readers and point a way forward for them in difficult times.

Two.   Good Grief.

I felt rather pleased with myself for inventing such a title to this chapter; but it was not long before I discovered that somebody else, when writing about bereavement, had already used it as a title for his whole booklet.

I was not a stranger to grief. For instance, when I went to Cambridge as a young man of 18 to take the entrance exams, on that first night away from home I wept bitterly, for I sensed that life in my boyhood home was coming to an end, and I was a little afraid of what lay ahead. It was the first time in my life that I was aware that the past must be laid aside in the light of new circumstances. Although there was no further situation quite like this, I was able to weep at times when I was going through stress and doubted my own ability to cope. That first experience was cathartic, for I never went through such a period of intense grief again in the years that followed.

Under normal conditions, however, I was much more phlegmatic Often in the evenings, while we were still living together, Eileen and I would watch TV. When we were watching a film or drama that became emotional, it was not unusual for Eileen to have tears in her eyes. By contrast, I remained completely dry-eyed, and she would look at me with mock criticism because of my apparent impassivity.

All that changed in October 2008. Eileen had had a careful examination at a hospital in Newtownards, at the end of which the two of us were summoned into a room to sit with a doctor and nurse. This made us somewhat apprehensive about what was coming. The news that Eileen had cancer in various parts of her body was devastating. When we got home, I went out for a jog. I did this not so much because I needed the exercise, but rather because I needed to bawl my head off; and as I ran beside the sea that is what I did. From that day onwards I have been in touch with my emotions in a completely new way.

Eleven months followed in which, though at times there appeared to be hope, the overall picture was one of steady decline. Finally came death itself. Eileen's life on earth was over, but my tears were not.

As Christians, should we not rejoice that our loved ones have gone to heaven? Are tears a sign of weakness? Far from it. We read of Jesus that, on approaching the tomb of his friend Lazarus, he wept. We nowhere read that he laughed, though some of his stories could have invited such a response. Jesus led a perfect life, and yet he wept. It is not wrong to cry.

Tears, then, have been a part of my life for the whole of the period since her death. They may be prompted by something specific – an object in the home that she appreciated, a place that she loved, a piece of music that she enjoyed and a host of other things; but they may also come without any prompting, and when they are not expected.

We tend to regard tears as something negative, and we try to comfort others so that they will stop crying and look more cheerful. We may even try to repress our own tears, feeling that this indicates a lack of trust in the Lord; but tears are a fruit of genuine love, and they are a necessary and helpful response to tragedy, so that we should not despise them. If we try to avoid them now, grief may break out in a more explosive way later on. In this chapter, however, I want to show how tears can be positive. That is why I have taken the liberty of calling this chapter "Good Grief".

Here, then, are eight ways in which tears may enhance our lives, whether they come from bereavement, which is our main preoccupation here, or whether they come from some other source.

(1)   Tears are a natural way of showing emotion.

On that first day when I received the devastating news about Eileen's condition, my first recourse was to share my grief with God. I went out for a run, as already described, because this was something that the Lord and I could do together. I poured out my heart to him, and so gained strength. It was not just a display of emotion: it was a plea for help.

Although, sadly, my running days are over, I find that walks can have the same effect. I am privileged to live by the sea. I can even believe that God had this in mind when he chose this house for us. I can therefore walk for a considerable distance without being in the midst of other people. These walks are journeys with God himself. Instead of being a mere introvert I acknowledge my helplessness to God and look to him for his consolation and his strengthening. I talk to him about how I feel, I pray to him for help, and this is sometimes done with ample tears to reinforce this.

(2)   Tears may lead to thanksgiving.

I find that often, when I am consumed by grief, I look beyond the grief to other things. I know that I cannot stay in the grip of negative emotions: there is need to counteract this with some reflections of all the good things God has done for me. The things which cause me sorrow need to be seen in the context of the whole picture. So on my walks I do not remain crippled by grief but start to thank God for my education, my health, my faith, my ministry, my practical skills, my friendships, my blissful marriage and everything else which has made life worthwhile. The tears are, in fact, a door that opens into something better. The grief in my life is not something all-consuming, but part of a wider pattern.

(3) Tears can be a form of confession.

Yes, my tears may lead to thanksgiving; but they may also have the opposite effect. I become more and more aware of my own failings. I recall things I have done wrong: although I have confessed them and received forgiveness, nevertheless I still feel tainted by them. Living in such a world as this it is all too easy to be tempted into further indiscretions. I still seem to be so far from my heavenly home, when sin will at last be behind me. Having tears left over from my sense of bereavement, I can use them to good effect by weeping for my own sins and imperfections. This is not being merely negative; for if I am ashamed of my sins, and am determined to put things right, there is more and more impetus to seek God's help in bringing me to a better place. Moreover he delights, through the Cross, to assure us of our complete forgiveness, no matter how heinous our sins and   failures may have been, and his ability to help us overcome them in the future.

(4) Tears can become a sort of prayer for others.

As I weep for my loneliness and for my sin, I still have some tears left over. My thoughts turn then to friends and relatives who are either without a knowledge of the Lord, or are not living lives worthy of the Lord. I think of them not in an attitude of self-righteousness but with a sense of real caring. I long that they may become all that God wants them to be; and when I see them a long way from achieving this goal, I weep for them too. Thus my tears have a good and positive purpose. Now that I have become a creature who is not ashamed to shed tears, I am able to do this with much greater scope and purpose than would be the case if I had not already been affected by my own bereavement.

(5)   Tears are an important stage in recovery.

Some people, especially men, think that to display tears is a sign of weakness. Rather than that, they bring emotional release that will help us to adapt to our new situation. Whether we grieve openly or on our own, it is a stage to be passed through if we want to get on with our lives. If we hold our tears back and try to pretend that everything is normal there may eventually be an explosion. There are books which tell us that our grief will last for a certain time: the average is three years. This does not mean, however, that there will be no tears after that. In a sense our tears will be there for the rest of our life, but we shall be able to cope more and more with our loss.

(6)   Tears are noted by God.

But where is God in all this? Psalm 56:8 tells us that God keeps a record of our tears. It does not matter whether we translate 'bottle', 'wineskins' or 'scroll': the main point is that our grief and its causes are noted by God. He is not a long way off, but he is close to us as we grieve. I recall a time when I was going through many painful situations in my ministry, mainly through the opposition that I faced.   The only way I could deal with it was to go into the church building and read through psalms in which the writer was going through similar problems; and in that situation my tears were part of the healing process. We can be assured that God is aware of our tears and can help us through such painful times, whatever the cause. In fact, out tears may have the positive effect of bringing us closer to God. Several people in the Bible, when their circumstances lead them to tears, find new strength when they, as a consequence, turn to God in heartfelt prayer. Even Jesus shed tears at the graveside of Lazarus.

This is how Graham Kendrick puts it:
"O Lord, your tenderness,
Melting all my bitterness,
O Lord, I receive your love."

(7)   Tears are a gateway to joy.

Another verse, often used at funerals, is Revelation 7:17:
"And God will wipe away every tear from their eyes". We
sometimes call this world a 'vale of tears'. But our residence
here is only temporary. When we get to heaven we leave all
our tears behind us. That is something worth looking forward
to. In that sense, when we attend the funeral of a Christian, he
or she is in a much better condition than those of us who are
left.

Of course, life is not all about grief. There are times when I
find I can truly rejoice in the Lord. To the non-Christian it
might seem strange that a person can grieve and yet also be
joyful; but that is one of the paradoxes of the Christian life.

Eileen Mitford, in her book, "Pathways to Joy", has a
section in which she imagines writing letters to her deceased
husband. I quote from this:

"Joy and sorrow, it has been said, are but different sides of
the same coin. That must be why my heart feels like this
these days – a coin that is constantly being tossed from
one side to the other.

Sometimes I am lifted up by such a surge of joy – as
though on the crest of one of those Atlantic breakers -
a joy so intense that I am almost ashamed to own it. Yet
I know it is God-given, like the touch of an angel's wing.
I feel myself bathed in the warm glow of a holy
presence.

But there are days when the waves seem to dash me

against the rocks, and I long for your touch, for the
comfort of your arms, the reality of your presence. My
throat aches with unshed tears, and I simply cannot
believe that you are gone beyond my physical reach..."
(page 137)

I can identify with that. On my walks by the sea, as I have
said, I sometimes find myself weeping, but at other times I am
full of praise to God. Sometimes also as I enter the gym, I get
on to the machine and start pulling the levers, and it is as if a
voice inside me accompanies these actions and cries, "Praise
the Lord. Praise the Lord."

Once, when listening to Dr Christine Baxter at the Bishop's
Bible Week, I took note of the teaching that there was a need to
rejoice in God rather than simply hanging on to him in my time
of trouble.

If there were only grief, it would be hard to bear; but the
two go together to make me a person more complete.

Simon Ponsonby, in his book, "More", speaks of the value
of wilderness periods in our lives. He writes:
"Wilderness is a place where God's people have less of this
world in order to gain more of God." (page 179)
Our wilderness periods, Selwyn Hughes suggests, comprise
failure, suffering, humiliation, bereavement, estrangement,
doubt and dereliction. It is amazing that God can bring so much
good out of sorrow; but, then, he is an amazing God.

(8)   Tears are the flipside of love.

Whilst tears may appear negative, they are a demonstration
of something very positive – the God-given love which we had
for the deceased. In the midst of our grief, therefore, we
can recall the beauty of that love relationship which we

formerly enjoyed and give thanks for it. In a sense, the greater our love, the more profuse our tears. Tennyson, with echoes of Samuel Butler, writes:

"'Tis better to have loved and lost
    Than never to have loved at all."

But it does not end there for the Christian. Whilst we know that we can no longer enjoy those mutual bonds here in this world, there is still the promise of renewing that love relationship eventually in a heavenly context. It is not the end of the story.

Three.   Lonely Days, Lonely Nights

It used to be the custom, when somebody died, to show visible signs of mourning by wearing black armbands, having a taste for black clothes, keeping the blinds drawn and so on. I remember the first funeral I ever took: as the hearse travelled through the town, men would doff their caps as a mark of respect. That would not happen now.

We are all familiar with the story of how Queen Victoria responded to her husband's early death. In her acute loneliness she stayed in mourning for the rest of her life. Such a display is not to be recommended.

When I was much younger we used to sing a chorus that ran
"No, never alone, no, never alone,
He promised never to leave me,
Never to leave me alone".
These lines were repeated, just in case we had not taken them in the first time. We sang them at boys' camps, beach missions and youth meetings I can even remember singing them in German at a youth houseparty near Koblenz. This was to encourage us when, as young Christians, we felt we were out on a limb. This was not really so, for God was with us.

(1) Early Days.

Although it is good to know that God is with us, we also relish human contact, and such contact is at its best in a good marriage. It felt good when at last I had a place to call my own; but it was even better when I was able to share it with my soulmate. This was to be a lifelong commitment. When all this ended, however, there was a great sense of loneliness.

I would sit in my easy chair, with its panoramic view of the coast, knowing that the other chair was empty. No longer would we comment together on this view that we both enjoyed. I wrote in a poem called "Beyond the Pastel Sky":

> These sights are now reserved for me alone.
> The companion chair now yawns empty and sad,
> for in this place there has been an untimely death
> without the subsequent flow of returning life;
> the colours, the sounds, the moving spectacle
> are simply the echoes of something that once we shared."

No longer would I go to bed, knowing that there would be a sustaining hug from my beloved before the lights went out. Suddenly I was alone in that bed. I now have a custom of sleeping on alternate sides week by week, but it is still only myself in a bed made for two. No longer would the two of us go on our weekly shopping expedition, but I would do a limited venture once a fortnight for the benefit of myself only, unless I was expecting visitors. No longer would we go together to the cinema or the concert hall, but most times I would sit there with an empty seat or a stranger beside me. No longer, on those coastal walks, would my hand be in the hand of another, but would more likely be in my pocket. It was a different way of living.

(2)   Communal Events.

For many people the problem is not having anyone to talk to. The house is silent, for there is no longer any verbal communication. The obvious solution is to get out more. I go to the gym regularly, and sometimes get involved in conversations with others there. I belong to various groups, mostly connected with mission or with writing, so that I can share with likeminded friends. Even on the day when I was preparing to write the first outline of this chapter, I went to pick blackberries, which could be a lonely occupation, but a friend who lives in that locality came out to help me, and I learned more about him that I had ever done before. At time when I am at home, I am never more than a telephone, a Skype call or a Facebook message away from others. It is most unusual for a day to go by in which there are no conversations, though I hear that for a million pensioners in the UK a whole month may go by like this. It may not be the same as those intimate conversations with one's spouse, but it can make life much more meaningful than mere silence.

(3)   The Value of Silence.

Some people talk with the absent spouse, just as if they were still there; as we have seen in Eileen Mitson's book, but the problem is you do not get any replies. For a Christian, the best plan is to talk regularly with God. Prayer does not have to be limited to a special slot, for God is available to us at any time. When I am walking by the sea and talking in this way, it may look as if I am talking to myself, but I know better. God promises to grant us the joy of his presence. The greatest benefit of this is that this is a friendship that will never die. Our loved ones are mortal, but God is eternal; and because of this we know that our loved ones who have died in faith are still alive but in another place. It is good also to know that the same God with whom I talk in prayer is also looking after Eileen in her new heavenly home.

We are never really alone if we belong to God. When Jesus was about to leave his disciples he said: "And surely I am with you always, to the very end of the age" (Matthew 28:20); and the writer of the letter to the Hebrews also quotes the words of Jesus: "Never will I leave you; never will I forsake you" (13:5b). Such promises can be a great comfort to us. The problem is that we do not always <u>feel</u> his presence. It is one thing to see a person physically and to talk with audible voices, but quite another thing to talk with someone whom we cannot see or hear in a physical way. I find that sometimes when I am out walking I am talking both with God and Eileen at the same time and almost getting them mixed up. But God understands. After all, I am celebrating the two greatest love affairs of my life.

(4)   Look Back with Thanksgiving.

There is a tendency for us to look back on times we have enjoyed together in the past and to regret that such times are over. A positive way of handling this, however, is to show a positive attitude of gratitude for those times. It is better to have communicated regularly with someone close to you and then to have lost them than never to have had communication of this sort at all. When we turn nostalgia into thanksgiving, we do ourselves a big favour. Although these things are in the past, they remain in our memories and in that sense they are still real. One advantage I have is that I have kept a detailed journal for most of my life, and all our encounters are featured there.

(5)   Bursts of Loneliness.

Sometimes the sense of loneliness has been more acute than at other times. During my first Easter without Eileen there are frequent references to this in my journal. On my first birthday without Eileen, I sought to thank God for the gift of singleness; but I had mixed feelings!
There were sometimes unexpected moments of deep emotion. I was watching an animated feature called "Up". It

began with a brief summary of the protagonist's life – his meeting up with his beloved, their happy life together, and then her early death. This resonated so much with my own experience and, though brief, it was sensitively and movingly done.

On the first anniversary of Eileen's death I received various phone calls from sympathetic friends and family. It was good to know that I was still loved.

On our first wedding anniversary since bereavement I visited the grave. I just felt I needed some sort of contact. But this did not become a regular feature in my life. In fact, I would not always recollect that it was our anniversary.

(6)   The Empty House.

Those of us who have been bereaved know all too well what it is like to come back to an empty house. As a young man, who had to share his house with others because I was single, I longed to be on my own, as I have already said, but all that has changed. When Eileen was still alive and well, after I had been out preaching, I would come back to find the table laid and a mug of coffee prepared for me. Now I have to do everything myself from scratch. It is not that I am incapable; but it still took time to adapt to this.

It does not help that my sons live far away in London, but there is no easy remedy for this: I could not afford to buy property in such an expensive locality. At least, we are able to visit one another from time to time, and these visits are precious to me. I would love to have the company of grandchildren, but at the time of writing all I have is a great niece in Blackpool. However, there may be possibilities in the future....

(7)   The Value of Friendships.

It is to be hoped that we have other friends to whom we can turn. Sometimes when a couple live so close together that others are excluded, the surviving partner feels absolutely bereft afterwards. Although other friends cannot take the place of a spouse, they are still people to whom we can relate. Whether they are close friends or just people whom we happen to meet, they keep us from that solitary existence that sees little meaning in the world around. One couple is kind enough to invite me to share an evening meal with them once a week. It is good to have groups of friends with whom we may go for walks, practise or listen to music, enjoy a drink, watch a sports fixture and so on. No matter how good these friendships, however, we still have to come back to an empty house.

(8)   Being Kind to Oneself.

When we are married to a partner whom we love, we like to be generous to one another. It is all too easy when we are living alone to avoid being kind to ourselves.

In the early period of my bereavement there was a friend who, despite a busy life, made time for me to visit her and pour out my feelings. One time we were talking about self-esteem. Later I wrote in the journal: "I have taken plenty of knocks, and at times it has been difficult to think well of myself. Now that I am alone, I have to learn to be good to myself and refuse to think that I am unimportant and undeserving because I am on my own."

Eileen and I would sometimes enjoy going to a coffee shop, of which there are many in Northern Ireland. Now and again I go to such a place and enjoy a piece of cake and some tea or coffee. At such times there is no need to feel I am being self-indulgent: it is what Eileen would have wanted me to do.

(9) Dispensing Hospitality.

There is a lot to be said for the practice of hospitality. If you feel you have the necessary skills, invite people into your home. They do not have to be the kind of people who will then invite you back. It means that the house is filled with voices again, and we can have the satisfaction of doing something which we trust is of benefit to others. In fact, giving hospitality to others is something commended in the scriptures. If, however, you do not have the skills to prepare meals for others, this is not a time for self-castigation: we are all different. You could always take a friend to a restaurant instead.

(10) Special Occasions.

There are special times when the sense of loneliness feels more acute. Rather than dealing with it here, I will devote a whole chapter to this toward the end of the book.

(11) Health Issues

For most of our married life, if illness struck, it was usually Eileen who would be affected. The good thing was that we were there for each other. Since being left alone, I have continued to enjoy very good health; but I have had my moments. At one time I had a painful back. At another I had a very sore thigh. I also had a bout of chronic toothache. At such times it was only too easy to wallow in self-pity. I needed the presence of somebody who would offer sympathy and understanding, but there was nobody there for me.

For some people, poor health is prevalent. To have to

endure this when there is nobody else in the house can be very difficult. In such cases, it would be good to have a neighbour who checks up on you each day. It is good also to have a device you can press if you are in trouble, that will summon help, thus alleviating anxiety.

For some people the issue is very different. We hear a lot these days about the problem of dementia. Most of us find that, as we get older, our memory becomes less sharp. The problem is to distinguish when this is normal and when it is a sign of the onset of dementia. If we have Alzheimer's, it can be very difficult for anyone who lives with us but they are ready to help us because of their love. If, however, we are living alone, we may become a danger to ourselves, and the only solution eventually is to go into care. It can be very difficult to distinguish between what is normal and what is a sign of illness. Sometimes we may grow anxious about our condition when there is no real need to do so.

(12) Thoughts of God's Care.

I began this chapter with a Christian song and I end with one One morning at breakfast I was feeling particularly lonely; then I listened to some music which Eileen loved. "Such love, filling my emptiness." It was the best thing I could have done. Yes, that was the answer to my feeling of being bereft. God loves us, whatever our condition, and he is particularly eager to demonstrate that love when we are passing through difficult times, especially when this leads us to confide all the more in him.

4. Hard Feelings

If you were to read only one chapter of this book, I would recommend this one; for it deals in detail with the effects of bereavement and how we can be helped to get over them. We shall also take a look at how friends can help the newly bereaved person.

Whether we like to admit it or not, we are creatures who have feelings. We do not go through life impassively, but as we move from one experience to another, so our feelings change. The most overwhelming event we have to face is the loss of a loved one; so it should come as no surprise to find that we are consumed by a variety of feelings, which we shall look at here.

Some writers suggest setting stages towards our recovery. One speaks of a cycle of numbness, pining, disorganization and recovery. Another mentions the five stages of denial, anger, bargaining, depression and acceptance. Others may offer their own lists. The truth is that we are all different, and one person's handling of bereavement may be very different from another's. The main thing is that there should be some positive outcome and a complete adjustment to the new situation.

Our feelings will vary according to our closeness to the person whom we have lost. They are at their most acute when we have lost a beloved spouse. The loss of a parent can also be traumatic, but we have always known that this would happen one day. I had to travel right across the world to attend the funeral of my father, who died at 68, whereas I was at my mother's hospital bedside when she passed away at 89, but both of these events were inevitable. It was just the timing and the circumstances we did not know about beforehand. The death of a child must be incredibly hard to bear as it is a harsh contradiction to the normal order of nature: thankfully, I have never had to bear such a loss, but I have had friends who have been devastated by such an event. The death of a grandparent may be easier to bear: I can remember as a small boy being told one day not to go near my grandparents' bedroom.. This was because my grandmother had died in the night. (Sadly my grandfather was so distraught that he took to his bed and refused to get up again and so ended up in a nursing home.) In the present day, there is sometimes a very close bond between the two generations. Here, however, we are looking primarily at the death of a spouse. Whatever our relationship with the person who has died, we may experience the reactions mentioned here, to a smaller or larger degree.

They may also vary according to our own character. Although we may face the same ultimate problem, the ways in which we seek to handle it may differ considerably. What I write in this section is based largely on my own experience, but there is nothing significant in the order, and nothing to suggest that all bereaved people must go through exactly the same reactions as myself.

We are often told that these difficult feelings should be resolved after one or two years, but we are all different. If we are little changed during that time we may need to look for professional advice; but for most of us many of these problems will have been largely resolved within that period.

(1) A Shock to the System?

If the death has been sudden and unexpected, the normal reaction is one of shock. We suddenly feel paralysed, and find it hard to make rational decisions. The worst situations must be after suicide, murder or accident. If, however, the death has come after a long illness, it is easier to accept it, as we have been preparing together for it. Such was my own case as I watched my wife's combat with terminal cancer. That does not mean there is no element at all of shock, but we knew it was going to happen, and that somehow made it easier to accept. If we are accompanying someone through a long illness this can be a journey of mutual support that has positive as well as negative effects. When death at last comes, it may bring much sadness but does not carry with it that deep sense of shock. At least, that was my own experience.

For some, there is a sense of numbness that lasts for the first few days of bereavement. In that condition it is hard to accept the new situation. The visits of friends and relatives may buoy us up, but after the funeral, for which we have sought to 'pull ourselves together' and when the visitors have all gone home, the reaction sets in. Some people may then withdraw from others, preferring to live simply with their own company. For some people it is like this, for others not. We cannot predict beforehand how it is going to affect us personally.

Some people, though suffering from shock, manage to disguise it and appear to be coping brilliantly with their situation. It is always possible, however, that underneath this there is some denial that sooner or later will have to be dealt with so that they may adjust acceptably to their new status.

That sudden paralysis, which is more normal, at its strongest when the death has been unexpected, is not likely to last for long. The immediacy fades. Gradually we shall recover the ability to cope with life and its demands. That time, however, varies with the individual. When the deceased has had Alzheimers's, there is less sense of shock, for in a way we have lost the real person much earlier, and there may even be a sense of relief, for which we must not be allowed to blame ourselves.

The friend who wants to help the bereaved in that state of numbness must be careful not to keep doing everything for them, but to allow them the freedom to begin to take back their own responsibilities.   .

(2) Look Back in Anger?

When we have lost somebody we loved, it is quite natural to feel angry. We must not blame ourselves, therefore, if for a time anger is uppermost in our minds.

It may be anger against people. If the doctor had acted differently, my loved one might have been saved. If that driver had been more careful, he could have avoided hitting her. If the country's leaders had not got involved in a misguided conflict such as the invasion of Iraq, a beloved son would not have been killed. The most extreme situation, however, would be that of murder, but not many of us find ourselves in such a situation. At the time of revising this, a 41 year old MP in Yorkshire has been brutally murdered. How must the husband feel? At the same time we read of terrible atrocities in many parts of the world. It must be incredibly difficult for the survivors to get on with their lives.

It may be anger against God. If God is completely in charge of everything, how could he have allowed this to happen? Surely, if he loved us, he would have kept my loved one alive. Again it is not unnatural to feel this way. God is tough: he can take our anger, for he knows exactly what we are feeling.

A friend who read my book, "Lark Ascending" said that he sensed I was angry after the death of my wife, but that it was not anger against God. I think that is true. For many of us there is anger without having any clear object for it. Anger is there, but it is not accompanied by blame.

If we are worried about the anger which is still there in our minds, we must first of all accept that this is a perfectly normal reaction to bereavement.

In their book, "Tracing the Rainbow", Pablo Martinez and Ali Hull write (page 12):

"Anger and protest are normal developments of grief. They express a desperate and unconscious effort to reinstate what is lost. Their outlet is an essential part of the healing process."

If somebody who has been more precious to us than anyone else is taken away, it is only too easy to feel angry about this, just as we would feel angry about the loss of anything or anybody that has been special to us. As Christians, however, we have the presence of a God who will never be taken away from us, and we can leave all our emotions, including anger, with him.

Friends may be upset when they witness such anger, but they need to accept that it is a normal stage of bereavement and not react too strongly. Under normal conditions, time will erase this problem.

(3)   Why Worry?

It is natural after bereavement to feel a deep sense of loss and a feeling of uncertainty as to whether we will be able to cope under our new circumstances. This is especially so if we have lost a beloved spouse.

This may affect us in terms of dizziness and light headedness. It may cause us to be apprehensive and fearful concerning the future. Will we be able to cope with the demands of living alone not only now but potentially into the distant future? What if we have to face illness and other problems whilst completely alone? Everything is unknown. Everything is beyond our planning and experience.

When the death has been unnatural or sudden the anxiety may become more acute and turn into post traumatic stress

31

disorder. In such a case help should be sought. For most of us, however, the anxiety is something we learn to live with.

For myself, anxiety has not been a big problem. God has given me the ability to cope with my new singleness, despite the distress involved. Although I have lost contact with Eileen, I have not lost contact with God. He is the one who bids me to cast all my cares on him, because he cares about me. I may not know what the future holds, but he knows. All I can do is to trust him for each step along the way, for he knows the whole picture.

There is a tendency for friends, witnessing such anxiety, to do too much for the bereaved; but it is good to encourage them to make their own decisions regarding the disposal of the deceased's clothing etc. It is good also to encourage that person to go out and treat themselves to tea and cake, or whatever small indulgences might give them some pleasure.

(4) Feeling Low?

Another reaction is that of depression. There is ordinary depression, which may issue in 'feeling low' and weeping. This may be compounded by a feeling that God is absent and that there is nowhere to turn for consolation. It is helpful to know that in normal circumstances that feeling will pass. God has not deserted us, but it is as if a cloud has hidden us from the sun, which is still shining out there.

Sometimes we may think about all those things we could have accomplished together if the loved one had still been alive. It can become a form of self-torture. Bit by bit we have to recall that it is not going to happen and simply give thanks for all that was accomplished when our loved one was still alive on this earth.

Depression can become more serious: it can lead to feelings

of unworthiness, a desire for self destruction, hostility in relationships, social withdrawal. Hopefully, these things will ease with time.

But there is also clinical depression, which is something more serious. If a feeling of depression goes on beyond 18 months after the loss and refuses to go away, it could lead to deep feelings of unworthiness, suicidal feelings, a false sense of guilt and even aggressive behaviour. If this happens, we may need to seek professional help.

Remember that grief is normal, but ongoing depression is not. Friends may be able to help by encouraging the newly bereaved to try new pursuits when the time is ready, but there is no need to rush. An unfeeling call, however, to 'snap out of it' is not going to help anyone

(5)   The Guilty Party?

Another possible reaction is that of guilt. Some people may look back to times when they have acted wrongly toward the bereaved. Now there is no means of saying sorry and asking for forgiveness. All they can do is nurse those feelings of guilt and hope that they will go away.

If the death is by suicide, this problem may be greater. We may look back on our recent behaviour and wonder if, had it been different, the loved one would still be alive.

If we are Christians we have a place to deal with this feeling of guilt. When Jesus died on the Cross our guilt was laid upon him. We can confess everything that lies on our conscience and experience the joy of being forgiven. It is just as if we had never done those wrong things.

Mostly it will be false guilt. We blame ourselves for the death, whereas in fact we did nothing to cause it.

We also have to learn to forgive ourselves if we are

conscious that anything has been amiss. We may receive God's forgiveness, and yet at the same time keep punishing ourselves for what we have done. Nothing can change the past. What is done is done. It is time to begin a new chapter. Basically, however, whether the guilt is real or imaginary, it needs to be brought to God for him to deal with it and restore some sense of peace.

Again, if the guilt goes on and on and never abates, we may need help from professionals. This may be hard for us if we are Christians, for we sense that confessing to God and receiving his forgiveness ought to be enough. But sometimes even that cannot bring us peace, and we may need to share our problem with someone who is qualified to help us.

(6)   Asking the Right Questions?

It is possible not to feel angry but to be full of questions. For instance, I felt that my wife was a better Christian than I was. If it had simply been a matter of justice, then I should have been plagued by illness and an early death, but it happened to Eileen instead. Why?

Some people may question whether, had they noticed the symptoms earlier and taken that person to the doctor, that early death could have been avoided.

Some may question whether they gave enough help to that person when he or she was alive. Whether they did or not, the situation is not going to be altered, so why plague oneself with such questions?

Some may question the love and the ability of God. Why did he allow this terrible thing to happen? Is he really worthy of our trust?

How easily we try to reduce it all to a matter of human deserving, whereas God's purposes are far beyond our understanding. All we can do is to leave our unanswered questions with him and get on with our lives.

(7) Any Physical Sensations?

Not all of us will experience these, but it is good to recognize them so that we know where they come form.

The list can include hollowness in the stomach, tightness in the chest or throat, oversensitivity to noise, a sense of depersonalisation, breathlessness, lack of energy and dry mouth. It is just the way the body reacts sometimes to a big shock, and these things, if they occur at all, should diminish as time passes.

(8) How Can Others Help?.

If you are not yourself bereaved and you want to help someone who is, what can you do in addition to what has already been said?

First if you are a family member or a friend it is good simply to spend time with them. You are not there to explain everything but simply to show love and acceptance and be a good listening ear. You must not expect immediate change but must be prepared for the long haul.

You are not trying to explain the reason why the loss has taken place, but if the bereaved person opens up you should give them a good listening ear and respond sympathetically.

You are not going to help by saying how others have dealt with these problems. We are all different, and such stories could make the sufferer feel more inadequate. Each bereaved sufferer has his own time for getting back to somewhere near normal.

You may notice that the bereaved friend is relying a lot on

medication. This may have been of some use as a temporary resource, but it should never become a regular habit. The mind needs not to be soothed by medication but to be transformed by inner healing.

(9) Getting Back to Normal?

In a sense we shall never get back to normal. 'Normal' meant living with the loved one, and that will never happen again. However, there is a new 'normal', when we resume as much of the old life as we can and fully accept that we have to cope now on our own. There may be agencies that help us, or we may move on without any such needs. Gradually, however, living without that beloved person becomes what our life is now about, and we have made all the right adjustments. 'Normal' means living how God wants us to live at each stage of our life. We have a better chance of such restoration if we have found sympathetic help when dealing with the problems along the way. But it is also good to pray as the Psalmist did in Psalm 31:15: "My times are in your hands".

Five.   Close Quarters

God created us primarily for fellowship with himself. He made us capable of entering into a close, personal and permanent relationship with him. When human sin interfered with this, he sent Jesus to bear our punishment so that we might return to him. But as well as relating to him, we relate to other human beings. This includes sexual involvement. That is primarily what this chapter is about.

(1)   God Made us as Sexual Beings.

It all started with Adam and Eve. If they had not been sexual beings, there would have been no human race. Sexuality is therefore God's good gift to us. At first Adam felt very lonely, and when Eve came along he felt a great sense of completion. From that time on, men and women have married, have enjoyed living together, have had loving sexual union and have produced children. That is what it normally means to be human, though there are some who feel called to remain single and still enjoy a fulfilling life.

In our own day we have demeaned the term 'sex', so that it is just associated with fun and lack of commitment; but that was never God's original intention. His purpose was that, in addition to giving a future to the human race, it should be an expression of deep love and commitment between two people. "It is not good for man to be alone." Sexual relations are for two people who are already married. and it is meant to give them plenty of enjoyment and satisfaction in giving expression to their love. To many people these days, however, suggesting that the sheer pleasure of sex should be kept for marriage partners would seem too restrictive an approach.

When Eileen and I got married at the advanced age of 35, neither of us had ever had sexual intercourse either with each other or with anybody else. This might be regarded by many today as 'medieval', but for us it was what we sensed God intended for us. This did not mean that there was no sexual activity during our courting days; but by God's grace we were able to delay any full encounter until our marriage.

Because of this, the week of honeymoon which we spent on the north coast of Ireland offered a steep learning curve. As the weather outside was cold and wet, we had plenty of time to work on this. And it was fun!

From then onwards, sexual intercourse was an important part of our life together. God gave us a love for one another which deepened as our lives progressed, and our sexual activity was primarily an expression of that love. Jokingly, when Eileen was ready for intercourse, she would sometimes use the Dickensian phrase, "Barkis is willing". Other couples might have a different way of putting it! Often after making love, we would talk together to God about it and even pray together, for somehow it brought us closer to one another and to him.

It was also through this activity that we conceived two sons, and it was a great joy for us to see them brought into the world in a Taiwanese hospital and to follow their progress from one stage of life to another.

We remained sexually active well into retirement, but when Eileen got very sick, that part of our life was gone forever. Our minds were still knitted together, but sexual activity was no longer possible. When Eileen died, then both kinds of encounter were a thing of the past. There was no longer a Barkis in my life. It was not an easy change to accept: all I could do was to be thankful for all the good years past.

(2) God Understands our Urges.

The problem is that I am still a sexual creature. If she were still alive, I do not think age would have deterred us from this delicious activity; but now it is no longer possible. I still have my sexual urges, and I have to bring this part of myself to a God who understands.

One morning, nine months after my loss, in my last doze before waking, it was as if Eileen came back to me. I held her in my arms, hardly believing that it was possible, and we spoke of our love for each other, just as we had done formerly. All too soon it was over. Maybe this was not unrelated to the fact that I was reading the 'Song of Songs' in my Bible studies at that time, and this has a lot to say about how we relate to one another as sexual beings.

If I still have these urges, that is perfectly natural, and I am not ashamed of such feelings.   The question is how (if at all) I act upon them as a widower.

(3) Looking for Another Partner.

Some people in my position would look for another spouse with whom they can enjoy a deep relationship. I have friends who have done this, and they have been happy. Such a new relationship may be limited to warm hugs, or it may embrace full sexual activity. There is nothing wrong with this, because death releases us from the obligations of the original contract. Nevertheless there are some people, such as myself, who still feel so committed to that old relationship that it is impossible to conceive starting all over again with another person. I do not discount the possibility, but I do not consider this as a very likely development in my case. I think age also has something to do with it. If I were looking for someone else with whom I might be involved sexually, then the best way of doing this would be would to enter into a new marriage contract. But at present I feel inclined to remain as I am.

(4) There Are Non-sexual Relationships.

We can still enter into simple non-sexual relationships, where mere companionship is enough. There is a woman whom I knew as a young girl when she was one of the children in a church club that I ran in my native Blackpool. After a long gap, I met up with her again here in Ireland. We invited her husband and herself over for a meal. One year later both she and I had been widowed. Occasionally we may go to a concert together, or I may go to a concert at which she is singing in a choir, for we both enjoy music. I have also met up with her at Christian conferences. There is however nothing more to the relationship than that, but it is good to have some companionship even on these very isolated occasions.

I also have an American cousin, who came over on a visit a few years ago. I took her to various parts of Northern Ireland, including Rathlin Island; then I took her round England to meet various cousins and to do a bit of sightseeing. At one place where we stayed they mistakenly housed us in the same room despite our request to the contrary. However, there was nothing sexual in our encounters: it was someone to talk to without any sense of threat. Nobody would expect such a relationship to be heading for marriage, but the temporary companionship was good.

It is not my contention that to stay alone is better: all I can do is describe my own experience and my own feelings. The Bible says we are free to re-marry if we get the opportunity. It is just that I do not feel this is for me.

(5) *Make the Most of What You Have.*

I must say that I enjoy chaste hugs, usually amongst Christian friends; but this is a completely non-sexual form of activity. It is, however, a physical demonstration of warmth toward another person that is perfectly permissible for us as Christians. That is one reason why I enjoy my visits to the Belfast Chinese Church and why I enjoy welcoming certain visitors at the door. Of course, we still need to understand the other person well, lest we should simply create embarrassment.

As for the frustration of no longer having a sexual partner, I am thankful for what I have enjoyed in the past, and now seek by God's help to keep myself clean.

But, of course, our sexual activity is really a demonstration of our love for each other. After losing Eileen's physical presence it did not mean that I no longer loved her. At the same time, I sought to show more love for others; and those chaste hugs are one demonstration of this.

Six.   Been There, Done That

I think people must have had a lot of patience with me when I was a raw young curate. I often found myself visiting people who were sick, who were elderly and infirm, who were bereaved and so on. I offered them sympathy, read the Bible and prayed with them, and they expressed their gratitude. Yet this was a world about which I knew next to nothing, for I was young and in perfect health and had no personal experience of these things. However, I did my best to try and understand what they were going through.

After my marriage, a new experience for me, it was easier to get alongside other married couples, because we had a lot in common. This was a positive development. When Eileen was pregnant, she ran classes for other expectant parents. When we became parents ourselves, we had a lot of fellow-feeling with others who were also parents. When we were returnees from the mission field we understood more the kind of culture shock such people felt who were in that position. When you have experienced something for yourself, you are in a better position to help others who are going through a similar experience.

(1) Exercising Ministry.

When I suffered the loss of my dear wife, I entered into a completely new period of my life. It was the severest trial of my whole life but the positive side of this was that it helped me to get alongside others who were also going through such a tragedy. The expression "I know how it feels" is not now mere empty words, but something heartfelt.

Paul has some helpful words for us. Although the context is

very different, I believe the principle is the same. He writes of "the God of all comfort, who comforts us in all our troubles, so that we can comfort those in any trouble with the comfort we ourselves receive from God" (2 Corinthians 1:5). So it is not just a matter of passing through an experience, but also of learning from God in the midst of it.

From the time Eileen became ill, I was honest and open with others about how I felt. I also shared, both in private and public ministry, how God was enabling me to handle the worst thing that had ever happened to me. It was not just a matter of sharing all that was positive, but also my problems and mistakes. This lasted all the way through her decline and on into the period of bereavement. I knew there were many in the congregations I served who were no strangers to such experiences, and I hoped that my honesty would in some way help them.

When I wrote my book, "Lark Ascending", it was not in order to make a name for myself, but rather to help other people to deal with the process of accompanying a loved one through the pain of terminal illness. It always gives me pleasure when someone claims to have read the book and to have found it helpful. The book has been a kind of extension to my regular ministry. I hope this second book about bereavement will also achieve a useful purpose.

Recently I was asked to speak to a small Christian group about my relationship with Eileen. I think they appreciated my honesty, and several of them bought my books afterwards. My only regret is that these books only reach a small handful of people.

(2) Receiving Ministry

Of course, it is not just a matter of sharing the experience of loss with others. The positive side is that God is able to help us in our times of loss and to manifest his presence more clearly to us. No doubt there are some people who manage to draw upon their own inner strength to help them deal with times of devastation, but that is not what it is all about. At such a time as this, I draw more than ever before on the consolation and strength that only God can provide. It is to that same God that I desire to point others.

It is not just one-way. Yes, I have more ability to minister to others now, but I am also open to any help which others may give me. Once, when I was visiting a spiritual life centre in Albany, New York State, and taking part in a big service there, I found myself given to tears, and I much appreciated the prayers of others for me at the end of the service.

(3) Sharing Ministry.

A group of us have for many years been in the habit of meeting for prayer once a week. I kept on attending even after Eileen had died. Another member of the group, who had a Kenyan wife, also became ill. His condition gradually deteriorated. I used to go to read to him, as he was no longer able to do this for himself. After he died, it meant there were now two of us in the group who had suffered the pain of bereavement. In a sense, it is easier to trust God when all is going well. "God's in his heaven, all's right with the world". But when things have gone horribly wrong we still have something to offer to which the non-Christian world is a stranger. Our intention is not to boast about how we are coping but to indicate that our strength comes from God alone.

As a retired minister, I am sometimes asked to conduct funerals. I have been doing this all my working life, but now I feel that more than ever before I can identify with the bereaved partner and point them to God. In that sense my ministry is more complete than previously.

A friend of Eileen's who had gone out with her to the mission field also died recently of cancer. There was no husband to mourn her, but plenty of friends attended the funeral who had known her over many years. I also attended, knowing that Eileen would have been there if she had still been alive, and was glad that I had done so. As one grows older, one is no stranger to the deaths of friends and relatives. It is not a matter of theory but of personal experience.

(4) Facilitating Other Ministries.

For the last six weeks of her life, Eileen lived in a Marie Curie hospice. Although she did not have the strength even to get out of bed, the nurses gave her drugs to alleviate the pain and were fully prepared to do anything, however menial, to make life more comfortable for her. After she died, I felt a debt of gratitude to the movement, so I have often taken part in street collections on behalf of the hospice work. The latest one that I did raised £112. I have also done sponsored swims for them: it is worth swimming for an hour and three quarters if Marie Curie can be richer to the tune of £400 or £500. Many of those who give to the project have themselves watched their own relatives receive that much needed palliative care.

Some people go further than this and volunteer their practical help on a regular basis to help organizations like this. They find that, in service to others, they gain much personal satisfaction. Life is not just about receiving, but it is also about giving. A lot, of course, will depend on our own health and our capacities.

(5) Jesus Understands.

There is an interesting verse in the story of the raising of Lazarus in John 11. It must be the shortest verse in the Bible, consisting simply of the words "Jesus wept".

In a way, this seems out of place. Jesus was about to raise Lazarus from the dead, so surely this should give cause for rejoicing. Yet at that moment, as we have already seen, he wept. Jesus understands what it is to lose somebody whom we love through death.

Now, when I weep for the loss of a loved one, I know that Jesus shares my grief. He understands the pain and grief of losing someone who is special to him. I take comfort from this.

Seven.   Say Something

In married life you are never short of someone with whom to hold a conversation. If you are both Christians, then you can enjoy good Christian fellowship and so encourage one another in your spiritual walk. It is also possible to talk of our shared interests, or even of our differences! I feel I am a better person because of such conversations when Eileen was alive. But the subject is wider than this. Let us start with the most important conversations.

(1) Praying Together.

It is good when husband and wife can pray together. It is true that we can attend church prayer meetings, but it is of particular benefit to pray with your spouse concerning matters which affect both of you, as well as touching on wider subjects, and this can be done at any time and in any situation.

This does not mean that all conversations are purely spiritual. When we were together we were able to share jokes, share our memories, make plans, talk of our sons, discuss books and dramas and so on. It was good in all these matters to have two perspectives rather than just one.

When you are left alone, all this changes. The house seems strangely quiet. If you have something important on your mind there is nobody with whom to share it. If you have a prayerful concern about some matter you have to pray alone, unless you can share it with others in a church meeting or an informal group.   I certainly value belonging to the little group that meets every Friday evening at our church, and our times of prayer can be very precious, but it is not quite the same.

However, there is something positive about holding regular

conversations with God. The walks which I used to share with Eileen I now share with God. Although we do not hear God's voice audibly, we can learn a lot from him through our reading of his Word, by which he also speaks.

(2) Means of Communication.

Of course, when we get out and about we meet up with all kinds of people, and if we are sociable creatures this will mean holding positive conversations with many of them.

In these days of electronic devices, also, it is possible through our smartphone, through Skype and chat rooms to converse with family and friends at any time, no matter where we are. For some people, however, the enthusiasm which they show when chatting with others on such devices is not matched by the poor quality of their conversation when face to face with others.

Facebook and Twitter and other such facilities are also popular in our own day. You type a few words, and maybe hundreds of people will read what you have put. It is an amazing phenomenon which embraces more than a billion people. I first began to use Facebook when my wife was terminally ill so that I could show others that there was life beyond the sick room; and those who have read my other book will be familiar with some of these contributions. After her death I decided I would continue to use this means of contact, for it encouraged me to take a look at each day and try to work out what had been most significant about it- a positive and helpful exercise. Now it is hard to imagine life without Facebook!

Through e-mails also it is possible to keep in touch with others wherever in the world they may be. Not many of us now write personal letters. We used to publish the letters of famous people, but I doubt whether books of their e-mails will attract publishers. We have learned to communicate quickly and efficiently, but have sacrificed some depth of reflection and some literary merit in the process. On the credit side, if there is a prayer need, we also have the advantage of being able to share it with a lot of people all at once.

(3) The Wider Context.

There is no substitute for good one-to-one conversation. The New Testament speaks several times of the virtue of hospitality. While Eileen was alive, we liked to entertain guests; and since her death I have sought to keep up this tradition. Fortunately I can produce food that is edible. Were this not so, then it might be a form of torture rather than hospitality. When we entertain others, it means that conversations are still taking place in the home, where those more intimate dialogues used to take place. It is a poor substitute, but much better than living in a place that is always silent. The downside is that we may be too busy in the kitchen to appreciate the whole of the conversation!

Just recently a friend came to stay for a few weeks while his visa application for China was being processed. We had plenty of opportunity for conversation, and even enjoyed Bible Study together in Mandarin. I think it was good for both of us. It was also good to learn more from him of the local bird life, which I had taken for granted.

(4) An Extended Prayer.

As I have already said, there is someone who is always there to give us a listening ear, and that is God himself. We are never alone if he is with us. The whole of life becomes an extended prayer, for we are in conversation with him for so much of the time. In a sense, being bereaved gives us an advantage, as there is nothing to distract us from talking with God. What is missing, however, is that three-way conversation which is possible when husband and wife both know the Lord.

(5) A Voice Beyond the Grave.

Before she died, Eileen left tapes for myself, for our sons and for a personal friend. I listened to mine at the beginning, but have not listened for a long time. It is some comfort, however, to know that I can listen to her voice whenever I want to; though I am aware it would probably produce a flood of tears. It was brave of Eileen to record these tapes in the first place, and I am glad that I still have the opportunity of listening to her voice. My sons and that personal friend also have similar opportunities.

Eight.   Doing Things Together.

Activities are much more enjoyable when we can share them
with another person. One of the joys of married life is that we
can share in a wide variety of activities with someone whose
tastes are perfectly compatible with ours or with whom we
have learned to share our each other's enjoyments.   When you
are left alone, the temptation is to withdraw into your shell, but
this is not a good idea. Here are some examples of shared
activities and the modifications needed after bereavement.

(1) Shopping.

There are some men who leave all the shopping to their
wives. Even when I was busy with parish work, however, I
sometimes took time off so that we could do the shopping
together. I have never regretted this. In retirement this
occupied each Thursday morning. First of all we drove into
Comber, where there was a farm shop, and there bought a lot of
organic goods. After this we drove together to what was then
the nearest branch of Sainsbury's, situated at a place called
Holywood. Then we would drive home with the fruits of our
labours.

When Eileen became ill, we could no longer go shopping
together. This was something I had to do alone, and there was
no guarantee that Eileen would be able to eat the food that I
chose. As there was a branch of Tesco's a little closer to home,
that is where I went to do the weekly shop. Although I missed
having Eileen at my side, I saw this as a bit of 'me-time', when
I could have respite from being a carer, even though it was only
for little over an hour.

After Eileen's death, I still needed to eat. I felt it was still important to give myself a varied diet, but I did not need to buy as much food. I therefore developed the habit of shopping only once a fortnight. In due course another branch of Sainsbury's nearer home was established and the organic farm shop moved beyond my reach to a more remote location. Because of these features, I was able to do the shopping in different locations from before, and this made it a little easier to bear. This regular shopping expedition is a necessary and a regular part of my current routine and it fits in with visits to the gym, a comparatively new activity of mine.

(2) Entertainments.

During marriage we have a regular companion to go with us to shows. When we are left alone, it is perfectly possible to go to these events on our own, but it is not quite the same.

Eileen and I sometimes went to musical concerts. Mostly these were free concerts given by the Ulster Orchestra for broadcasting on Radio 3. Occasionally, however, we would attend smaller concerts in other places. Since my bereavement I have continued to go to the Ulster Hall, but on my own. For smaller concerts, however, as I have already written, I have sometimes taken a friend with me.

Occasionally we would go to the theatre. Since I was bereaved I have gone very seldom; but not often alone. One time I went to see 'Ruddigore' in Belfast with a male friend. Another time I went to a play in London with one of my sons. One Christmas I went to the theatre with both sons. Such visits, however, tend to be the exception rather than the rule.

Sometimes we would go to the cinema. I still do this, but usually alone. When, however, my sons come over for Christmas, we usually go to see a film together - often the sort of blockbuster which I would personally have avoided!

Although the enjoyment of such pleasures is enhanced when there is someone to share them with, it is not essential, and I find I can still derive plenty of enjoyment from them. And if there is nobody to discuss it with afterwards, there is still the journal and Facebook.

(3) Gardening.

In our last parish we had a large garden, and most of the heavy work in it fell to me. In retirement we simply had a yard, where we kept tubs and troughs, filled with flowers, and for which Eileen had most of the responsibility. In May we would go to a garden centre to select new flowers for the summer. Going there alone was not easy, but I wanted to keep up the standards. In due course a new garden centre opened with more reasonable prices, so that I was able to shop there without the nostalgia which the old venue carried with it. I sometimes wonder what Eileen would think of the new place: I think she would have liked it, especially as it is run by Christians and it includes a good coffee shop! I do not think the tubs and troughs in the yard look as attractive as they did in Eileen's day, but there is still a good splash of colour in the summer.

(4) Walking.

Eileen and I did a lot of walking together. When we lived in Devon, we walked the whole of the South West Coast Path, and I have written about this elsewhere in a book called "The Coast is Clear".   After our move to Northern Ireland we decided to tackle the Ulster Way. It was not always well marked: at one stage we even got lost in a forest and at a later stage we got absolutely soaked on our walk to Portrush. The next stage of our walk would have been more complex, owing to the hills and the lack of B&Bs, but it never took place.

Since Eileen's death, I have not walked a lot – apart from the regular half-hour walk near my home. I tried a bit of walking near Westport and got lost, drenched and exhausted. I did a church walk that involved going to the tip of the Ards Peninsula and back, but found that rather tiring toward the end; so I was glad to give up after 23 miles and get a lift for the last three. I also did a few days of walking on the Welsh coast with my wife's sister's husband and that proved enjoyable. This, however, has not been a major feature of my present life, though I am happy to find myself still fit enough for such activities. One day I simply walked the 9 mile stretch along the coast from Holywood to Bangor and greatly enjoyed this. I have sometimes contemplated further walks, and am beginning to bring this into effect.

(5) Dancing.

One thing I have never greatly enjoyed is dancing, for I am not very good at it. Once when we were doing a chaplaincy in Tunisia a woman who held dancing classes invited us to take part. I told her I was not very good. At the end of our session she told me that I was right!

Despite all this, however, I could enjoy a waltz or something that was easy enough for me. At the family wedding reception I attended a few months after Eileen's death there was dancing, but I could not face it, and retired to my room. On another occasion our church organized a barn dance, something I would happily have attended in the past, but emotionally I could not take it. Dancing is about two people, not one, and that is why I am now not so comfortable with it.

(6)   Christian Meetings.

As we both belonged to the Overseas Missionary Fellowship, we would go to their meetings regularly. For me, there has been no change in this. In fact, so many of the people who attend are good friends that it is rather like being with family. I therefore attend the days of prayer and I mostly go to the monthly prayer meeting, I have other other connexions with the mission too that will be described in Chapter Ten.

Church attendance has not changed very much. Eileen and I imagined that after retirement we would actually be able to sit together in church; but it did not work out that way. I was asked to take services in other churches; but Eileen remained in our home church so as to continue our commitment to it. Worshipping in different churches was not our preferred option, but that is how it worked out. Now that I am alone, I still take services in other churches. I attend some weekday events in my home parish and get to the occasional Sunday service, but I am not always quite abreast of what is taking place.

In the distant past, Eileen and I used to attend Spring Harvest. Now I go to New Wine at Sligo. Eileen would have loved it, but, sadly, she is not here to try it.

(7)   Other Groups.

In the early days of our retirement I used to go to a reading group, but Eileen stayed at home. After a while this folded up. Since Eileen's death I have joined a writers' group, where I have made several new friends. I have also joined a gym, which I attend two or three times a week. Quite apart from the question of fitness, it brings me into contact with other people.

I have also other friends with whom it is possible to exchange visits from time to time.

(8)   Reflections.

So where does this leave us? I think the main lesson is that we must not allow our bereavement to leave us buried in obscurity. It is important that we continue to meet up with others and to attend functions away from the home, so as to preserve as normal a life as possible.

If our bereavement takes place before the end of our working life, then the very routine of returning to the work to which we have grown accustomed can be helpful. There is still something left that is normal.

There is a lot to be said also for keeping busy even when we are at home a lot alone.   I am fortunate in that I have sermons to prepare nearly every week, and this for me is a meaningful and worthwhile activity. I am fortunate also in that my main hobby is writing, and I find that this pursuit makes my daily life very meaningful. Since self-publishing has become more accessible, I have managed to bring many of my books into the public domain, even thought the number of people reading them is low. The first one, which concerned Eileen's terminal illness, was for long the most read, but that has been matched by a book about Irish missionaries.. It gives me a sense of achievement if what I write is read by even a few. It enables me to feel that life has more to it than simply reading and watching television on my own. Most people reading this would not wish to attempt writing books, but sometimes writing something down, even if nobody ever reads what we have written, may help us to analyse our own thoughts and to deal with our problems better.

Another lesson I am learning is how to cherish myself. It

was what Eileen would have wanted. In fact, she herself told me I should do this. Just because I am left alone, it does not mean that I do not matter. One morning, for instance, I took a bus into Belfast, bought myself some new shoes in a sale, bought two new CDs, had coffee and a pastry and then caught the bus home. It was an enjoyable 'me-time'. When I have to visit my bank in Newtownards , as I have already indicated, I sometimes treat myself to coffee and cake at a well known coffee shop. Yes, it is all about cherishing myself – after all, that is all I have got left of the partnership!

Nine.   Home Base

The word 'home', as opposed to the word 'house' can be quite emotive. It is not just the place where you live but the place where you belong. Even that is temporary, since our real and lasting home is in heaven. Nevertheless we attach a lot of importance to the place on earth where we are currently living.

(1) Homes Down the Years.

When I lived in Taiwan, the word used for 'home' in Chinese was almost synonymous with 'family'. Home was where you lived with your nearest and dearest. After a period as a bachelor, I was happy, then, to be living there with my wife and my sons. This was indeed our home, and at that time it happened to be a Japanese bungalow. However, if you lived alone, the word 'home' was not considered appropriate.

When we came back to England and started work in a Wolverhampton parish, we lived in what must have been one of the smallest vicarages in the diocese, overlooking a cricket field exposed to the danger of having a ball smash through the window. When I started a travelling job with a missionary society, we moved across town to a house which a friend had bought and rented out to us. When we had cut down half of the 22 trees, there was more light in the house itself. Through these years we continued as a family of four and our sons attended a secondary school just down the road. In due course we moved to a small vicarage in Torquay, and our sons spent a lot of time away at university. When we moved to a rambling rectory in North Devon, only our older son, who had initially asked to stay for a week or so, was living with us. Finally, being directed by the Lord, we came to live in a house for the first time owned by ourselves, here in Northern Ireland, with a marvellous sea view, but there were only the two of us. Yes, there were family visits, but basically this was a home just for two. It is amazing too to reflect on how God made this provision for us.

We were very happy together here. This was the place God had prepared for us, and we were content to see out the rest of our days here if that was his choice.

What neither of us could have foreseen was that Eileen would die so early, and that 'home' would become something very different from that Chinese concept. However, I feel that this is the place where I belong. After coming in from the outside, I shut the door, and still feel glad that I am at home.

(2) Caring for the Home.

But homes do not look after themselves: there is work to be done. It needs hard work to ensure they are kept clean and tidy. We liked to work on it as a couple, for we both took a pride in its appearance.

When Eileen got sick, and was no longer able to do her share of the cleaning, the family suggested that I should employ a woman to clean. This I did, and that enabled me to give myself full time to Eileen and her needs. After a while she was replaced by a friend of hers. When Eileen died, I was prepared to let this woman go; but the family suggested I should keep her on. In the end, I compromised, by employing her one week and doing the cleaning myself another week. This worked well. Recently she handed over this responsibility to her younger sister.

I have known some men who, on being widowed, have lost all interest in the appearance of their house. For me, however, there are two considerations, apart from my own love of neatness: one is that I am a steward of what God has given me. To keep a clean and tidy house in some way honours him. The other consideration is that I like to keep the house as Eileen would wish to see it. I see no reason to lower standards just because I now live here alone.

In many years of parish visiting, it has sometimes not been very pleasant to visit the home of a widower. The carpets are stained, the shelves are cluttered and there is a smell of neglect. I recognize that for some men, they lack the skills and energy, or even the will, to keep the house neat; but I sense that there are others who have allowed the house to fall into disarray as a part of a larger scenario: they have given up on life. If the home meant such a lot to us while we were together, is it not fitting to try and keep it this way? I would like to feel that if Eileen were suddenly to return she would be satisfied with what she saw.

There are other duties beside cleaning and tidying. One of these is cooking. We all have to eat. Some men simply live on takeaways, which are not normally calculated to have a beneficial effect on one's health. Others buy ready-made meals which just need to be heated up. For me, however, cooking is no problem. My wife and I used to do this together, so it is not difficult to look after myself. I try to give myself a balanced and varied diet that will be good for my health. Since I am alone, one piece of cooking can sometimes keep me fed for several days. I have also started baking cakes and biscuits. In 2011 I baked my first Christmas cake, and this became an annual event. I have every incentive to look after myself in this way, for God cares about me and my wife, when she was alive, cared about me. Why should I not, then, care about myself?

We liked to regard our home as a place where others could feel welcome. I like to think I can still extend the same hospitality to others. Indeed, it would seem selfish to keep a clean, tidy and well stocked house only for my own benefit, even despite the considerations I have just aired. In any case, it is good to enjoy the company of others rather than to live as a recluse.

(3) Changes in the Home.

By 2010 it was obvious to me that the walls were looking a bit shabby, and some painting needed to be done. I got some painters in, and, instead of the magnolia walls, I had the living room painted green and the wall by the stairs a deep red (as used to be the case at 10 Downing Street!). I was not living in a museum, but in a place that belonged to me and could legitimately reflect my tastes.

Twice since then the living room has suffered leaks, and I have relied on the insurance for repairs and redecorating. However, the room has not changed in appearance.

Sometimes there are major decisions to be taken. When gas arrived in my area for the first time in early 2013, I had to choose whether to change to this from oil. This would mean installing a new boiler and incurring a lot of expense. There was nobody to discuss it with. However, I felt that Eileen and I would have decided together to change to gas, and that is what I did. I have never regretted the decision. It is cheaper in the long run, and, besides the convenience inside the house, it has also freed up an extra part of the yard where the oil tanks used to be.

Other than this, I have moved some of the pictures around and put some of the ornaments in different locations, with further changes every so often, but basically this is still the house that we once shared.

(4) Out in the Yard.

Having dealt with the house, I now move on to the garden. This is a subject already mentioned in the last chapter. When we had a vicarage or rectory, I usually had to do a lot of gardening, especially the mowing. The present house, however, has not a big garden but a yard. Eileen took it to her heart. And, as I have indicated, we made the place colourful through tubs and troughs of flowers. It is certainly much easier to look after these than the large and neglected garden at our last place. My problem is that I do not always know which are viable shoots and which are weeds, so I tend to err on the side of caution. This means that the yard is not quite as attractive as it was in Eileen's day. The garden also cannot normally be seen unless you are visiting our premise because of the walls that surround it. .Sometimes I take one of the troughs to the cemetery and place it on the grave so that a part of Eileen's garden is, in a sense, still with her. I have found this to be a very meaningful activity.

Sweeping the yard is also a regular activity, for so much waste gets blown in. Weeds also have to be removed from the cracks.

When the weather is good enough, the yard is also a place to relax. There, sheltered from the wind, I can read and enjoy a rare bit of sun. It is possible to get a tan even in the weather conditions of Northern Ireland.

(5) A Home for Others.

Much of the time here is spent on personal projects: I prepare myself a good meal, light a fire, and enjoy an evening of viewing. Since I had promised Eileen that I would cherish myself, I felt good about this.

Most of the time I live alone; but I sometimes have guests to stay here. Mostly these are family members; but I once entertained a South Sudanese bishop and, as I have said, a missionary friend stayed for a few weeks while waiting for his new visa.

I like to feel that others, when they visit here, can feel happy and relaxed.   Several people have remarked that the place is like the Tardis – apparently small from the outside, but big when you get inside it. Some people gasp when they enter the living room and get a glimpse of the sea view. Yes, I am very fortunate to have such a lovely home and to be able to share this on occasions with other.

Although home is where I live and nobody else, it is also a reminder of the happy life which we shared together, and anything that extends that must be good. It is also a place which my sons can visit and so experience what remains of our family life.

Ten. Living Church.

I am sure I would have found handling bereavement much more difficult had it not been for my Christian faith. My own individual faith has stood the test, and it has added strength to be a part of God's worldwide Church. Here are some thoughts about what difference it has made being a part of God's Church.

(1) Regular Worship.

When I was in full time paid ministry, my wife and I enjoyed worshipping in the same church building, but we could not sit together: I was at the front leading the worship, and she was among the congregation. That is one of the drawbacks of regular paid ministry, unless you can persuade your wife to get ordained too.

On retirement, however, it looked as if all this was going to change. For the first six months, we tried various churches in order to find out where God wanted us to worship. In the end, we concluded that he had put us in Millisle for a purpose, and that the local Anglican church, St. Patrick's, was where we should make our spiritual home. For a while this worked.

However, there were times when I was needed to play the organ for the service; and occasionally I was asked to lead the service and preach. It was thus by no means true that we could sit together all the time.

Before long the situation changed again. A parish not far away was without a minister for three years; and so I found myself conducting worship in its two churches Sunday by Sunday as well as visiting people in their homes. Eileen continued to worship at St. Patrick's, where we belonged, and she headed up its missionary committee. It could be said that the situation had deteriorated: not only were we not sitting together, but we were not even in the same church.

When Eileen died, I was just beginning to work in two other churches. Actually, I appreciated having opportunities for ministry when my situation was tough, for it gave me some normality. It also gave me opportunity, as I have indicated, to share exactly how I was feeling. Sometimes my pastoral work would take me to hospitals where Eileen had spent time as a patient, but I managed to distance myself from any nostalgia that might have troubled me. The hardest one to visit was City Hospital, where she had been placed when her cancer was acute.

Some Christians, when they are bereaved, take some comfort by regarding their local church as their 'family'. Where there is mutual love and regard, this can work very well. Our little church in Millisle was too small to hold the congregation for Eileen's funeral; so we used our sister church at Carrowdore, to which the burial ground which we would be using was attached. About 200 came to the service, which was conducted by the then Rector, whilst the Bishop, who had been very supportive, spoke. There was definitely a family feel. But I also found that my friends from other churches where I had ministered had gone through the experience of caring and loss with me, so that I did not feel alone. I also derived a lot of comfort from continuing in ministry in the churches I was then serving. There was never any question of taking a break so as to give me time to recover.

My own situation, then, was unusual. For most people it is from the members of their own local flock that the bereaved person feels deep love and sympathy. Knowing that our grief is shared throughout the whole congregation, for they too have known the deceased, takes away that feeling of isolation. Being part of a family, where there is a strong element of faith, helps us to to see that life still has direction. For myself, though, there was fellowship from people in various churches.

We had benefited during Eileen's illness from the love and care of our local minister, Kevin, and from the Bishop, both of whom, as I have said, were present too at the funeral service. However, not long afterwards Kevin moved on to another parish, and Colin, a new minister, was instituted. Strangely, he had also married an Irish wife and moved over here from Devon. Now we had a local pastor who had never known Eileen, but who had enough problems of his own. But time moves on, and I had to accept this.

(2) The Wider Church.

I have also valued going from time to time to the Belfast Chinese Church to preach. It means a lot to me to meet up with a lot of young people, with a lifetime of service before them, and to make some contribution to their lives. As the Chinese people had been so important to us both, it has felt good to be working with them even at this stage of my life. I even minister to students from Malaysia. After language study in Taiwan, I was meant to work with the Church in Sabah, but could not get a visa. Had I done so, I would never have met Eileen. The Lord has his plan. Now, however, I meet up with students whose home is in Sabah. You could say that I went there the long way round. Although I am known to the four congregations more than Eileen was, there was one time toward the end of Eileen's life when we were both able to minister at the Easter conference, and that felt good. Recently I became a trustee of that church.

As well as our commitment to local churches, Eileen and I

were members that successor of the old China Inland Mission, the Overseas Missionary Fellowship, now locally known as OMF International.   We had served with this missionary society, and, since moving to Northern Ireland, had been regular attenders at local OMF events. This region was a more self-contained community than the regions in England would be, and there was definitely a family feel. When there were two of us we were part of that family; and when I was left alone I was still a part of that family.

Since Eileen's death, I have actually had more to give. I found myself chairing the group of selectors that would judge whether candidates should be sent overseas: it was both a privilege and a responsibility. I was also involved in the group that was planning events to celebrate 150 years of the mission and was asked to write a little book about it. From time to time I also host the OMF Prayer Group at my home. All this has created an even deeper sense of belonging. It is good too to be amongst folk who remember Eileen with great affection.

(3) Large Christian Gatherings.

Sometimes Eileen and I would attend large Christian events. A few times we went to Spring Harvest in Pwllheli, Minehead and Skegness. We would go to the OMF conference at Swanwick. After our move to Northern Ireland we attended the latter only occasionally because of the distance involved. We did, however, go to the local OMF conference each year. Each time it felt good that we could enjoy these occasions as a couple.

It was some time after Eileen's death that I became aware of New Wine conferences in Sligo. I have now attended these several times. It is a lively conference, with enthusiastic singing and opportunities for personal ministry, which I think

Eileen would have appreciated if she had still been alive. When invited to go forward for ministry, I am often slow to respond; but I sense that Eileen would have frequently taken advantage of this. She would probably have sought a place on the ministry team also. Although it means going alone and living in a room by myself, there have been are often plenty of our church members there, and I have not really felt alone. On my latest visit, however, these were few in number and this made a difference.

In 2015, instead of this, I went back to the Keswick Convention, with which I had been familiar long before I met Eileen, and noticed how much it had changed in the intervening years. This time, however, I knew very few people and there were not a lot of personal friends to meet up with. After all, these people represented the whole of the UK.

(4) A Place of Refuge.

Although Eileen and I did not attend large conferences in the latter stages, we were very much attached to the Christian Renewal Centre in Rostrevor. The resident members there accepted us gladly when we went to give our services for domestic duties. Cecil Kerr, who had founded the place, had been a good friend, but, sadly, had developed dementia in the last few years of his life. After Eileen's death, it was to this place I went for quiet prayer and consolation. Not long afterwards, however, the building was sold to Youth With a Mission, and it was no longer for me a place of refuge. I went to the closing ceremony and wrote in my diary: "I was very close to tears, especially during the singing. I knew that Eileen would have enjoyed singing these songs and wondered how she was enjoying the worship of heaven. I reflected too that we would never again stay at the centre together to help with the chores. It was the end of an era."

Whilst it is perfectly possible to know God's comfort when we come to him alone, and, basically, for each one of us it is the personal walk of faith which is the most important, there is much to be gained from meeting regularly with God's people in all manner of contexts. I am glad, therefore, to be a part of these various churches and of the missionary community, for they are indeed the Christian family to which I now relate.

It is good to know that we are part of God's Church. This means not just the people who are alive right now, but also those who have already passed on to the next life. In that sense, Eileen and I are still part of the whole, even during this time of personal separation. During our journey through this life and into the next, we know that God is with us: "the Lord will watch over your coming and going both now and forevermore" (Psalm 121:8).

Eleven.   This World's Goods

This morning I was ironing the sheets. They belong to the double bed, where Eileen and I once slept together. This reminded me how most things in this house were once owned by the two of us, but now belong to myself alone.

This leads me to reflect on the subject of 'possessions'. We bring nothing into the world, but it does not take us long to accumulate plenty of goods. You have only to look at a small child's play room here in the West; and that is only the beginning. As we grow older, we accumulate more and more, and it can become a problem knowing what to keep and what to dispose of.

We are told in the Bible that our life does not consist in our possessions: there are much more important things. It is just that we in the West tend to have too many. Nevertheless we all need some possessions to get by.

When a spouse dies, then what is left behind is a combination of shared possessions and his (or her) personal possessions.

(1)   Personal Possessions.

One of the first decisions, after a spouse's death, concerns what to do with the clothes. Some people keep a few of their spouse's clothes just as a reminder. I did not see much point in that. Eileen's clothes therefore went to a charity shop right at the start. Eileen's sister was kind enough to do this for me when I was away on a break. What amazes me is how my own clothes now cover both sides of the wardrobe instead of just half! Others tell me they have the same experience. I have, however, kept some of Eileen's jewellery, though not by conscious choice, even though I have no particular use for this. Some of the best of this had already been removed, while Eileen was still alive, by a burglar, so there was not a lot left.

There was also the question of Eileen's bicycle. At Instow we had both bought new bicycles, and had enjoyed traffic-free rides on the Tarka Trail; but here the roads were busy and Eileen had not used her machine even once. I found that a new friend of mine had a teenage daughter who needed a bicycle; so I passed the machine on to her, and the money which I received for this I gave to the church.

There is still in the attic a box containing her memorabilia, and I have not yet dealt with this. There are also a few small notebooks of her writings, which I have no intention of throwing away. I also came upon a box full of study material supplied by Clinical Theology to train her for pastoral counselling. As this was no longer of use to the family, I regretfully threw this away, apart from a section which I thought might provide some extra material for this book!

(2) Shared Possessions.

If I go round the house, I see so many reminders of Eileen. When the house was being prepared for occupation, I was still living in Devon, and Eileen and her sister Betty did most of the planning. There are many stories about this. We needed tiles for our bathrooms. One day Betty was wondering about this while she was driving. Suddenly she saw a notice that said, "Tiles this way", She followed the directions and came upon a sale in which tiles were going cheaply. Should she or should she not buy them on our behalf? She did so, and we were very grateful to her. These and many other features of this house are the product of planning done by the two sisters.

There are still many examples of their careful provision. I

have to confess that not much in the preparation of our house for our living here came from my own inspiration, as I was busy with parish work in Devon; but I am very happy with what I find here and very grateful to both of them for setting it up and thus giving me this great legacy.

(3) A Tour of the House.

If I make a tour of the house, I come upon so many reminders of Eileen. Does this simply fill me with nostalgia? Let us take the tour and see.

I am typing this in the study. It was built as a small bedroom, but is ideal for this other purpose. This is the one room that entirely bears my own stamp; but I have hung on the wall a small photograph of Eileen taken at Chris's wedding which reminds me how beautiful she was.

I move to the spare bedroom, which also served as Eileen's study. This has become more and more my own preserve. On the wall hang photographs of scenic places, all taken after my bereavement. I have replaced two paintings that Eileen owned with family pictures taken during our Taiwan days, but this could be subject to further change. In the main, this room does not now carry so many distinctive memories of Eileen, though I have only to open the sewing drawer....

The next room is the master bedroom. This room is full of memories. In retirement, Eileen took up painting, and there is a large seascape which she did hanging on the wall. Over the bed there is a large cross stitch depicting butterflies. This too is a skill which Eileen acquired in her later years. For the most part this room recalls Eileen's occupation, including the chair where she sat to pray daily. The bedclothes all date from her time. The lilac shade that predominates here was her own choice of colour.

I go downstairs to the living room, and again I see much of Eileen's influence there. When the building of the house was being completed, Eileen insisted that there should be a fireplace where we could burn coal.; but after it was installed, and we had moved here, I was the one who had to do all the hard work. Although on my own, I still light fires there on winter days and enjoy the warmth and the cosiness of that setting. Maybe the most poignant feature is the two easy chairs. We used to sit here, gazing at the coastal scene through the window, and comparing viewpoints. Here too we held many delightful conversations. I quoted earlier a part of a poem which I wrote about this.

This room also contains the television set which I bought during Eileen's illness to enable her to enjoy her programmes in a better way than the old set afforded; there is also the piano, which we were both able to play, but which was more my own preserve.

The kitchen always says a lot about the woman of the house. Here are the pots and pans, the designs on the tiles and the many vessels which she bought and used. Cooking, however, as I have said, was something we shared together, so these things do not only remind me of her: they are also part of my own life and experience. Of course, some utensils have needed to be replaced since my loss. That is inevitable.

There is a small utility room. Originally it was not supposed to be a part of the house, but we asked for it to be added on, and did not regret our choice. When I use the washing machine these days, acquired to replace the original one, there is a lack of feminine garments.

The hall has not changed very much. It is still dominated by rows and rows of my personal books; and the chaise longue, which was Eileen's choice for the new house, is still there on display.

(4)   Mode of Transport.

In this area it is helpful to have a car, as the bus routes are
somewhat limited, I can remember going with Eileen to a
dealer in Barnstaple in 2002 after a kind friend had offered us
an interest free loan to buy a new car. We chose a Honda
Civic, as Japanese cars were supposed to be reliable. We both
enjoyed driving it. A few months later, when we retired, we
drove it in one day all the way to our new home. Here it would
normally normally parked in the yard. I took pleasure in the
continued use of it for a long time; but the proximity to the sea
had caused it to get rusted, and eventually the time came to
abandon it for a new car. I was surprised at the sadness which
this prospect brought me. I found myself going back in my
mind to that day when in Barnstaple we chose it. However,
nothing lasts for ever. The necessity to abandon things we
have owned together is another thing which I find hard to face.,
but we cannot hold on to things simply because of nostalgia.

(5)   Frequent Reminders.

Possessions, possessions, possessions! I could, of course,
open drawers and cupboard doors and come across other things
that speak of her – a diary in which she made spiritual
comments toward the end of her life, a notebook in which she
wrote poems, needle and thread for sewing, books about
painting.... Do I need to go into any more detail? Occasionally
I open some of her writings and read, but I do not make a fetish
of it.
I have opened at random a notebook in which Eileen
recorded her thoughts from time to time. This extract comes
from the period just before her cancer was diagnosed, when we
had been on a visit to St. Andrew's, Chorleywood:

"We spent the whole day praising God and pressing into his glory. As we did, I felt a real burden to pray for the Ards peninsula which the Lord cut across and said that through the praise he had broken the spirit of death over the peninsula. We were to go back and declare this and start a Peninsula Praise at Greyabbey."

We did so, and these gatherings, in various parts of the peninsula, are now a part of our ongoing spiritual life. Eileen was able to attend the first one, held in Greyabbey, through the use of a wheelchair.

After Eileen's death I took off my wedding ring, as I was no longer married. Two years later, however, I slipped it on again. I was not planning to marry anyone else, and I liked to think that in a sense we were still bound together.

To summarise, our character is very much present in the things we cherish. By doing this tour, I recall so much about Eileen and the sort of person she really was. No doubt others, after bereavement, will make a similar tour. But it is not just about making a tour. These things leap into our gaze whether we are looking for them or not.

(6) Seeing This in Context.

The Bible tells us that our life does not consist in our possessions. These are all temporal things, and after we die they will no longer have any significance for us. Life consists not in possessions but in receiving the gift of eternal life. That which is temporary will fade, but that which is eternal will remain. It is pleasant to be surrounded by things that we love and treasure, but we should still see all this in the light of eternity. I am trying to reduce the number of books on my shelves, clothes in my wardrobes and relics in the attic.

My wife no longer has need of those things which she

accumulated here on earth. One day my own goods will no longer be under my control and what to do with them will be somebody else's problem. It is the same with all of us.

There is also a challenge about how we use our money and possessions while we are still here on earth. Do we use them just for our own enjoyment, or do we share them so as to help others? The world is full of need: if we enrich ourselves while others are in desperate straits, how can we be at peace with ourselves? The goods we acquire for ourselves will still be around when we can no longer use them; but what we give away can benefit others long after we leave this planet. The generous person will be remembered with affection long after death has claimed him.

(7) Temporary Possessions.

As Christians, we do not regard our possessions on earth as permanent. Of course, we want to enjoy a pleasant and comfortable life, but there is something else beyond. That is the subject of the present section.

I have already described the various homes in which we lived and what they meant to us. I have looked at our possessions. The purpose of this section is not to give a further description of these but to look at them in the context of the heavenly home which is promised we shall inhabit one day. This does not mean that looking after our earthly homes is not important, but we must learn to have a biblical perspective.

Most of our homes were temporary: they went with the job, and we could not claim to own them. It was only the home we moved into upon our retirement to which we could claim ownership. Usually we would take our possessions with us when we moved; but when it was a major move we even got rid of most of these. And yet this last move was at the time in our lives when we were closest to moving on to a place that could truly be called our permanent home.

(8) Our Possessions in Heaven.

We lived in each of our earthly houses for a limited time and then moved on. However, there is one home which I have not yet begun to occupy. It is a home to which Eileen has already gone, and where I shall also join her one day.

This new home, which we call 'heaven', is so different from the other ones. You can't go to take a look at it in advance, you can't see pictures of it on the internet, you can't measure the rooms ready for moving in and you can't take any of your possessions there. When we were moving from our home in Wolverhampton to Torquay, we were parked in a layby when the removal van drove past us. It was odd to reflect that in that one van were stored all our earthly possessions. Now Eileen has already left all her worldly possessions behind her, and I shall do the same. The removal van that time will be empty.

As Christians, we have the assurance that a place is waiting for us in heaven. It is the place, above all, where God lives, and where we shall experience his closeness. It is the place where we shall have a reunion with our loved ones who have gone there before us.

Nobody has seen heaven and come back to report on it. Some people, however, have what is called a 'near-death experience'. There was a time before I knew Eileen when she ate cold chicken at a wedding and became very sick, so much so that she was hovering between life and death. It seemed to her that she was about to enter heaven, and there to welcome her was Nessie, a fellow missionary who had died early in her overseas service. It was all so real; but she came back to earth, and some time later the two of us met. If she had not come back, I would never have known the joy of her presence.

It ought to bring me a lot of comfort to know that one day I will be reunited with Eileen in heaven. Indeed, we often comfort the bereaved by reminding them of such a promise.

(9) Current Limitations.

The problem for me, however, is that I find it hard to picture heaven. What does it actually look like? What will our loved ones look like in their new state? Will they resemble the one whose body we placed in the ground, or will they look different?

I don't think I am alone in finding it difficult to embrace the reality of heaven in my personal thinking. I tell people it is something more wonderful than anything we have ever known; yet despite the passages of scripture that deal with it, it is still something quite outside my experience. My imagination has difficulty taking it in and this affects the quality of my expectation.

I believe in resurrection. I believe that Jesus' resurrection was a kind of 'firstfruits', to assure us that we too will enjoy a life beyond this one. I believe that our current possessions will seem as nothing compared with our heavenly ones. For the time being, however, this is in my thoughts and emotions rather than in my experience.

All I can do is reflect on some of the thoughts that come into my mind as I read the scriptures. My first thought is that God desires the best for his children. He does not want to make us disappointed. We can trust then in the goodness of all his promises.

Sometimes I look at those things in this world which bring me the greatest delight and then reflect that these are just small pleasures when compared with the blessings that will be ours in heaven. When I look at it this way, although I do not have a concrete picture of heaven, yet at the same time I know that it is something that is infinitely worth looking forward to.

A few days after Eileen's death, a friend reminded me of a poem she had written:

"Yet a little while -
trust me, my child -
and you will run and skip with me
in the glory of the morning."

This moved me to tears.

One Valentine's Day I wrote in my journal, "In this time of separation Eileen and I are bound together not just by our own deep love but by the love of God for both of us in our very different situations".

One Sunday, on my way to conduct a service at Greyabbey, I found that some words of a hymn came into my mind:

"More happy, but not more secure,
When glorified with him in heaven."

Currently we live by faith; but one day faith will turn into reality. The days of imagining and waiting will be over. We shall have entered into our eternal home and begun to enjoy our heavenly possessions.

Twelve.   Separated.

One of the great delights of married life is being with a person whom you love above all others. Some people boast that throughout their marriage they have never spent a day apart, but for most of us there will be separations, even if they are very brief.

(1)   A Temporary Separation.

It is sobering to reflect that I have not seen my wife for seven years. As we used to love to spend time together, the absence, as I have indicated, has been hard to bear.

For a few years I had a job connected with China ministry that involved a lot of travel. Occasionally this would mean travelling to the Far East and being away for as much as five weeks at a time.

I remember well the first time I did this. When I reached Heathrow to catch my flight, there was a considerable delay. As I sat there in the airport I was sorely tempted to go back to the train station and return home; but, of course, that was out of the question. We both found such absences hard to bear; it was only the knowledge that we were doing God's work that enabled us to go through with it. Usually it was Eileen who was at home and myself who was away. There was one occasion when I was visiting our old home in Taiwan; but Eileen heard the news from me when she had neglected to put the clocks on for 'summer time' and had arrived for church at completely the wrong time. I could tell she was on a 'downer'.

It was not always myself, however, who was away. Occasionally Eileen might go to Ireland to see her family at a time when I could not make it. Toward the end of our time in

Devon she would make visits to Ireland to work with her sister on setting up our retirement home.

What made such absences easier to accept was the knowledge that it was just for a limited time. We both knew that on a certain day we would be together again and could make up for lost time.

(2) An End to Separation.

This time of separation is so different. We have the promise that one day we shall be together in heaven, and without such a prospect the situation would seem very bleak indeed. What I do not know, however, is the date when this is going to happen. I could be here on my own for many years yet. We do not choose the time of our own death: that is for God to decide.

It is wonderful to know that we have eternal life, so that we shall never die eternally. To belong to God both in this life and the next is an immense privilege; but it is still necessary to live out my life within the span of years which God accords me here on earth. Even while we are living alone on this earth he promises us the assurance of his presence here and now to sustain us.

There is an additional thought that what for me is a time of separation will not appear that way to Eileen, since she is outside of chronological time. She has been spared the pain of a lonely life, which I have had to face down here on earth. In this respect I am happy for her. We both have a great reunion to look forward to.

(3) The Drawbacks of Separation.

During this time of waiting, I am blessed with good health. I am well able to do alone those things which we formerly did together. What I do not know is whether this good health will continue. If my health should deteriorate, with my family living a long way from here, I would either have to cope on my own or make a difficult decision. When Eileen was ill, I was there beside her at all times; but if the same should happen to me, neither Eileen nor anybody else could be there for me on a regular basis.

It is foolish, however, to worry about things which may never happen. God is able to keep me in good health. If at some future time he chooses not to do so, then he will show me what alternative arrangement will come into force. God does not deal with hypothetical problems but with actual ones. All the same, as those living strangely separate existences must to admit, there is a lot of uncertainty to be faced.

Even if good health continues, there is still the necessity to have to do everything on our own. In the past we could pool our gifts; now we have to be omnicompetent. If we are fortunate, there may also be friends and family who have particular gifts that help to make up for our omissions.

(4)   No More Separation.

However much we may have loved that person who has died, there is a greater love open to us all, and that is the love of God himself. It is a different kind of relation ship since, while we are living on earth, we cannot see him. Nevertheless, if we truly know him we can be assured that there will never be a time of separation. I like these verses from Romans 8:

"For I am convinced that neither death nor life, neither angels nor demons, neither the present nor the future, nor any powers, neither height nor depth, nor anything else in all creation, will be able to separate us from the love of God in Christ Jesus our Lord" (vv. 38-9).

Thirteen.   On Holiday

Some of the happiest times Eileen and I spent together were our holidays. In the spring and autumn it was not unusual for us to take a sunshine holiday, mostly on Spanish islands. We also travelled more widely when we spent time in the USA and in Australia visiting friends and sightseeing. These were great times of sharing in the lives of friends from the past whom we still loved.

When I was left alone, all this changed. There was no longer a ready-made holiday companion. How would I handle this change? This chapter, which will be longer than most, examines how I sought to continue to take meaningful holidays without my beloved companion. Each section deals with a different kind of holiday. For some readers, this may provide some good ideas; for others it may have little to say. We are all different.

(1)   A Clean Break.

For eleven months I had remained by Eileen's side during her illness.   There were no holidays: it was simply a matter of being together every day during this crucial period. When Eileen was taken, all this changed.

When we used to do holiday chaplaincies, one place we hoped to go to one day was Cyprus; but it never happened. However, I had some friends who had property there, and they had invited me to go over some time. After Eileen's death, therefore, I decided to make immediate use of this opportunity. This would represent a complete break from the demands of those long months.

The funeral had been on 28 September. On 7 October I was

on my way. It so happened that some neighbours of mine, who also had property in Cyprus, were travelling out at that very time. This meant I could travel with them and even stay overnight at their flat so that my friends, who could not do night driving, could pick me up the next day.

It was a time simply to relax and to put behind me the trauma of the past year; though I could not help recalling that it was exactly a year earlier when Eileen had been taken ill while holidaying in the Algarve. We made some expeditions, including one to a castle which sprawled up a mountain slope and another to a remote peninsula, where my friends kept a caravan. Oddly enough, the church where we worshipped on Sunday had as its pastor a man whom I had known when he looked after a church some 20 miles from my home in Northern Ireland.

It was only a week's holiday, but for me it came at exactly the right time, and being with friends helped me in my time of adjustment.

(2) Lone Occupant.

I wondered what it would be like to go on a seaside holiday, but without Eileen. When I was offered a cheap holiday in Tenerife, I decided to take it. February 2011 therefore found me back on the island I had formerly visited with Eileen, though in a different region of it. Even before I got to the airport, however, I found I was full of misgivings over taking this trip alone. I enjoyed the winter sunshine, and was happy to lie on a beach reading a Jeffrey Archer novel, punctuated by dips in the sea; but it did not feel the same without Eileen.

Every evening when I went out to eat, I was the only one going out alone: the others all went as couples. One evening I met a couple from Poulton, near my native Blackpool, and ate with them, but that was an exception. And when I got back to my accommodation it seemed odd to have all those facilities just for myself alone. It only seemed to accentuate that sense of having nobody close to me any more. Somehow I felt that this type of holiday was no longer a lot of fun. My journal expresses how painful the experience was for me, despite the pleasant surroundings.

(3)   Visits to Friends.

   A different kind of holiday was visiting friends who lived in the British Isles. Shortly after the trip just described, therefore, I went to visit a friend in Bray, County Wicklow. This was a new area to me, so it contained no memories. Together, we visited an old monastery in a scenic area, the village where 'Ballykissangel' was filmed and an old jail that had become a museum.

   A few months later I decided to visit Devon, where we had lived for many years and stay with friends. The difference this time was that I had to face many memories. Such memories, however, rather than being regarded as nostalgic, could actually be cause for thanksgiving. First I stayed with a family friend, who herself had no relatives, and who had therefore much appreciated our friendship in those far off days. This also enabled me to revisit my old church in Torquay and to meet the clergy couple who were now working there. I also called on another clergyman and his wife who had been good friends in those days. Then it was up to the north coast to the parish where we had ended our ministry. There was opportunity to take a look at our old home, bought by a merchant banker and substantially altered for the better. My son Chris (who was on a short visit) and I were able to look through the windows but not to go inside, as the people were away, but we could see that it was much altered for the better. Merchant bankers have more money to spare than the Church of England.

The following Spring my cousin from New Jersey came over to see me. We visited Rathlin Island, known for its wild life, and enjoyed a visit to the RSPB centre, where the puffins, unfortunately, were not easy to see, as they were huddled together well below in the shadows. After crossing over the water, we called on various family members in England. We also visited Bonsall, where our ancestors had lived for hundreds of years, and were even invited inside a house on Puddle Hill where they must have dwelt 400 years earlier. We also visited Cambridge and explored the Fellows' Garden at my old college. The great advantage of this arrangement was that I had a female travelling companion without any suspicion that I was trying to form a new relationship. After seeing her off at Heathrow, I spent several days slowly travelling west and north, calling on various other friends before catching the ferry back to Northern Ireland.

More recently, using 'plane, trains and coach, I visited, amongst others a couple from my Cambridge days now living in Newport, a couple from my Wolverhampton days now living in Bristol, various folk in Torquay and a couple who lived near Southampton. These were meaningful encounters, but there was also time to explore bird life and historic houses.

(4) Family Visits.

There have been, of course, frequent visits to London to see my two sons and to Blackpool to see my brother, my two nieces and my great niece. And these visits were reciprocated. These were family relationships, most of which would continue. With my two sons I also made visits to the Matlock area of Derbyshire and to South Crosland, near Huddersfield, in order to walk where our ancestors once walked. I was glad of the opportunity to help my sons to understand something of the family's past. It is one thing to study old census forms, but quite another to be in the very environment which was theirs.

(5)   People in Exotic Locations.

There has been some opportunity also for foreign travel. Two of these trips have been sunshine holidays. A Christian couple who have a chalet on the coast near Bordeaux had invited me to visit them, and I enjoyed doing so. At another time a group of Christian friends were due to spend some time in holiday accommodation in Fuerteventura, so I was able to join them. It was good to get my ration of warm sunshine in the company of other people, and not alone as had been the case in Tenerife.

Another time my son Chris and Judit invited me to go to Budapest to spend time with her parents. The visit coincided with a national day, so there were crowds everywhere and a dramatic firework display. When Eileen and I had made a brief visit to the city several years earlier, we were robbed, and our projected visit to a spa was abandoned; so this time I made up for it with a happy time enjoying the spa facilities. We also spent time at her parents' second home beside a lake. It is good to have so many new memories on which to reflect. I also spent a few days' holiday in Northern Italy in the same company in the late summer of 2016.

There were also three longer trips. One of these was to the USA and Canada. The main reason for going was to join a party from our diocese visiting the Diocese of Albany for their annual conference. On arrival I went to visit a couple we had known in Taiwan. Before the actual conference we stayed at a spiritual centre where Eileen and I had once stayed. That was not so easy for me. The conference itself was good and uplifting. After the conference, whilst other delegates from Northern Ireland flew straight home, I visited Canada (mainly Toronto) to call on various friends whom we had known in my Taiwan days; then I travelled by Greyhound bus to Indianapolis to visit a Chinese convert from those same days who was pastoring a congregation there, spent some time with a retired pastor in Holland, Michigan, and finally visited my cousin in New Jersey who took me on a visit to New York. The best thing about this trip was the opportunity to renew acquaintance with so many old friends.

On another occasion I travelled with Chris and Judit to Beijing and to Taiwan. As this was where I had first met Eileen and where we had lived as a family for many years, it was a special event. I took my son to visit the hospital in Changhua where he was born, but even I would not have recognized it now after so many years. Eileen loved Sun Moon Lake, but our trip to it this time was overshadowed by Chris's bouts of vomiting! At least, the monkey which had grabbed his leg there as a small boy was not to be seen. The house where we had lived in Tainan was no more, and even the hostel beside it would shortly afterwards be pulled down. We got to it only just in time. The only drawback for Chris and Judit was they they had to spend such a lot of time being entertained by my old friends rather than being free to explore.

The longest journey was a visit to New Zealand and Australia to meet up with old friends from Taiwan days. On the way out I stopped at Singapore, and, as I walked through the Botanical Gardens, I reflected that Eileen must have often done this when she was based at our international headquarters for fourteen months just before I got to know her. In New Zealand I stayed with a friend whom I had led to Christ in his student days. Now his wife needed regular dialysis. His son ran a travel company and gave me a free coach trip over many days with a group of people from Mainland China. This even included a helicopter flight over Mount Cook.

Oddly, when in Australia visiting a Chinese couple whom I had known when they worked in Taiwan, I stayed at Eastwood, the same suburb of Sydney where Eileen's relatives had formerly lived, but now it was full of Chinese and Koreans. At that time I did not know I had any relatives in that country; but on this occasion I enjoyed a picnic with 50 of my own distant relatives, all the progeny of a great great uncle.

A shorter trip than these was a coach tour in Turkey. As it was out of the normal season, it was offered at a big discount. There were 33 of us altogether, some married and a few single. We were of similar age and background, and soon struck up good friendships. Whilst exploring sites mentioned in the Bible, it was good also to have such congenial company, and I would recommend the experience. It was among the more positive ventures I have entered upon since my bereavement. Sadly, since then the country has become more dangerous and tourism must have seriously declined.

In all of these trips I was rarely alone, but enjoyed the company of friends and relatives.

(6) Going for a Walk

One of the things that Eileen and I greatly enjoyed was our coast path walking in the south west. Over an eight year period we walked the whole of the 630 miles between Poole and Minehead. Afterwards I wrote a book about it called "The Coast is Clear". They were amongst our favourite holidays.

In the summer of 2014 I decided to do some more coast path walking, this time with my wife's sister's husband, but in a different setting. We travelled to Dublin and took the ferry to

Holyhead. Over the next few days we walked along part of the
Welsh Coast Path in the Lleyn Peninsula. On this holiday I
was able to recapture the joy of such walks without having to
do it alone. I also travelled further back in time to the days
when, as a student, I used to help at a beach mission at Nefyn,
and we visited several places that spoke to me of those distant
days. In all, however, I have not done a lot of serious walking,
and I am wondering whether I should do more of this in the
future, and, if so, where.

In the meantime I have enjoyed that afore-mentioned three
hour and twenty minute coastal walk from Holywood to
Bangor, and this was most enjoyable.

(7) Christian Conferences,

As I have written elsewhere, sometimes Eileen and I would
go to Christian conferences. Conferences I have attended since
Eileen's death I have already described, so I will not repeat
myself here. It is sufficient to say that these also were holidays
with a purpose, and there was always opportunity to enjoy
fellowship with others.

*

All this may sound complex. For me the main benefit of
travel, since I found myself alone, has been meeting up with
friends. I have also not lost the capacity to enjoy new scenes.
Yes, there is life beyond those twice annual shared warm
weather holidays. I have got used to boarding a 'plane alone
and sitting with strangers. It is not ideal, but I accept that this
is what my current life is like. If I remained all the time at
home, I would be depriving myself of some of the real
pleasures which even widowers, whilst good health brings

freedom, can enjoy.

Some people who are widowed manage to strike up warm friendships with similarly placed folk, and it then becomes possible to go for holidays together. This has not happened to me, but I have no regrets. I can still travel with the Lord.

Fourteen .   Facing the Music

Music can be highly emotive, especially in these years of bereavement. I think it is worth devoting a whole chapter to the subject.

For Eileen and myself, music was always important. We enjoyed listening to good music whether on tape or on CDs, and had built up a good collection of spiritual and 'classical' music, with a little jazz as well at Eileen's request! At times we both sang in choirs: I particularly remember a performance of Verdi's Requiem in Wolverhampton and concerts that mainly featured the music of Rutter in North Devon. After we had sung Rutter's Requiem, the audience remained quiet in a sort of reverence brought on by the quality of the singing; and only then did they clap. We were both able to play the piano also. To sum up, without music, our lives would have been so much the poorer.

Now when the house is silent, music performs another function. When there is no prospect of conversation, music can perform a welcome function of turning silence into something richer. As I consider this, however, I find there are three particular functions of music.

(1) Reminders of Life Together.

There are pieces of music which immediately send me into the past, for they remind me how we enjoyed them when we were together. We were both very fond of 'Gabriel's Oboe' from the film, "The Mission'. Now whenever I hear it again there is a temptation to leave what I am doing and simply to listen, just as if Eileen were still with me. I was almost tempted to play that music at the close of her funeral service.

This is not the only piece of music that is emotive in evoking memories. If I hear singing from the Verdi work already quoted, I can imagine the two of us singing with that choir all those years ago. It is the same with some of Rutter's pieces

Sometimes we would attend concerts of the Ulster Orchestra, especially those performed in a special series in July and August; and now when I go alone I think back to the times we enjoyed this experience together.

Eileen had a beautiful singing voice. This came out in particular when she sang an old Irish folk song called 'Lark in the Clear Air'. In the earlier book I mentioned how we played a recording of this at Eileen's funeral; and whenever I hear this song, no matter who is singing it, I am taken back into Eileen's presence.

(2) As an Aid to Worship.

We both enjoyed worship songs. There were plenty of old hymns, but we also liked bright modern worship songs. We particularly liked the songs written by Stuart Townsend, for they combined good music with sound theology, and we were able to worship from the bottom of the heart. Such a hymn was "In Christ Alone", which Eileen chose for her funeral. There are other hymns which had not even been composed in her lifetime, but which I think she would have appreciated. One such is "Ten Thousand Reasons" by Matt Redman and I cannot take part in the singing of this this without my eyes filling with tears and my hands being raised in the air as we sing "Bless the Lord, O my soul...." So it is more than nostalgia: it is a positive experience of opening my heart to the Lord.

But there are other worship songs that capture my heart. One of them, like the one just quoted, is also by Matt Redman.

This is a song which Eileen found it hard to appreciate, but it is important to me. We sing:

"Blessed be Your name
in the land that is plentiful,
where your stream of abundance flow,
blessed be your name.
And blessed be Your name
when I'm found in the desert place,
though I walk through the wilderness,
blessed be Your name."

Yes, I walk through a wilderness that I do not understand and my eyes fill with tears; yet it is as I bless the Lord that I receive the strength to go on. We do not always understand why God does certain things, but we can still praise him.

Another worship song that is filled with meaning for me is Keith Getty's "There is a Higher Throne". I am reminded of a joy beyond my current tears as I sing:

"There is a higher throne
than all this world has known,
where faithful ones from every tongue
will one day come.
Before the Son we'll stand,
made faultless through the Lamb;
believing hearts find promised grace:
salvation comes."

How can I remain downcast when I embrace such a hope? And it is made all the more exciting when I think that Eileen will enjoy this future experience with me.

(3) Simply Playing upon the Emotions.

Sometimes, however, there is music which does not revive memories, nor does it lead me into worship. I think of Craig

Armstrong's evocation of the balcony scene from "Romeo and Juliet". Whenever I hear it, I often have to stop what I am doing and simply listen – unless, of course I am driving. It is not a piece which we listened to together, and yet it deeply moves me, as it speaks of the quality of true love. Although it saddens me, I feel enriched simply by listening. Music is such a positive feature in my life, and I would be so much the poorer without it. I think also of Smetana's 'Voltava'. When I hear this, I think of how we celebrated Eileen's 70th birthday by taking that cruise along the Czech river. Another time-honoured piece is Bach's Double Violin Concerto. I am also deeply moved by Barber's Adagio for Strings. h Maybe it is my nature, but it is sad music rather than uplifting music that draws me most. That does not mean, however, that music cannot also bring me joy and lift me above my circumstances. Sometimes a piece of music can instil in me a sense of delight that nothing else would be able to accomplish in the same way. Yes, the world would be so much the poorer without music.

Fifteen   What's New ?

As with our holidays, in our ordinary lives too we need to do some rethinking. It is no use living in a time warp. Rather than grieving over the things we can no longer do together, it is good to embark on some new adventures. Here are some of the new things that I have tried since my loss in addition to the holidays already described. They are not necessarily the things God may lead you to do, however, for we all have our different skills and interests.

(1)   Using Our Gifts.

Each of us is different. Every one of us has his or her special gifts and abilities. For me the main such gift is writing. Ever since I was a boy of 9 at primary school this ambition has figured large in my mind.

Over the years I have written much, but published little, apart from the occasional article or story. In later life much of what I wrote was read by Eileen only: often I would show Eileen something I had written and she would appraise it for me. When we retired, writing occupied a bigger portion of my life than it had ever done before.

When Eileen died, the first thing I felt led to do was to write a book about those last few months we spent together. Self publishing was just coming in. The result was my book, "Lark Ascending". Even now it gives me pleasure when people I do not think I know very well tell me that they have read the book. It enables me to speak to a wide circle of people.

But that was only the first. I published memoirs on Kindle of my service life, my experiences at university and my seminary years and am preparing one on my first curacy in

Blackburn. I was surprised to find that I had so many bouts of depression during that last period, and wondered how much that might have been alleviated if I had already been married to someone like Eileen. I also published two novels in that form and a book about my visits to China. I published in softback a travelogue about our walks on the South West Coast Path, but it contained errors that I had not altered, so I was less eager to distribute it. In both Kindle and paperback, using Amazon, I published a book about worship and a novel set in Taiwan. For OMF I wrote a little book about some of our former Irish missionaries. This was followed by a book expounding the epistle of James, with stories from the Church in China. This particular book I had written while Eileen was alive, but could not find a publisher for it; now I had undertaken a revision of it and I was pleased with the result. All this was very fulfilling. It was not that writing was a new experience; but finding a way to publish what I had written certainly was. This current book is merely the latest in the series, and there are more to come, including a book on experiencing God's guidance. There is such a lot of stuff in there waiting to come out. Not many people know of my books or read them, but I am pleased to make contact with others in any way I can: it is better than simply bottling everything up inside my head.

As well as writing these things myself, I sought the company of other writers, and joined a group that meets in Holywood once a fortnight. This gave me another circle of like-minded friends.

Having been dissuaded by the talents of other writers at Cambridge from writing poetry, I decided at this stage of my life to take it up again. The first poems were an expression of what life was like without Eileen, but I soon turned to other topics and discovered that I had a talent for poetry after all, even if it was only a second class one. If Eileen had still been alive, we could have compared poems.

My poem 'Departure Lounge' , which I conceived on my
way back from New Zealand, has some connexion with the
theme of this book:

"Once you have got through 'security'
it begins with expensive perfumes,
jewellery and other such luxuries,
but then gives way to cups of coffee,
books to prepare you for your journey,
and signs to tell you where to catch your 'plane.

In life too we have to make our choices
between the luxuries and the things we need;
we come at length to the departure lounge,
with a few last trifles to engage us,
but what matters is not the departure gates
but the final destination that awaits."

Writing may not be your gift, but it could be there is
something else to which you are now able to give more of your
time and which will help you to feel fulfilled.

(2)   Exercising our Bodies..

All through our lives exercise is important. We may not be
Olympic athletes; nevertheless we all have bodies, and if we
treat them well there is a good chance that we shall have a
better quality of life in our later years.

For most of my life, running has been very important to me.
Every morning I would go out for a run before tackling other
responsibilities. I even did six marathons.

Shortly after my bereavement one of my sons, as a gift,
purchased membership of a tennis club, and I valued the
company of a new group of friends, as well as the opportunity

for further exercise. As well as playing, I found myself doing h
exercises with them and attending their social functions.

It was a blow when the doctor told me that, because of knee
trouble, it was not advisable to run any more. The same
restriction applied to my tennis. This hit me hard: it was like a
further bereavement. I wrote a poem about it which ended in
God's imaginary address to me:

"Just come to me, child, because there is nothing to fear;
for soon you will come to a place that has been prepared,
where no longer the cries of loss and frustration are heard..
Once here, you will run, leap and dance in great measure
and this will be simply the start of that higher pleasure
which I have prepared for those who have run the race
and have passed beyond to the joy of a better place."

However, this led me to join a gym: I now go there two or
three times a week, and it has become like a second home to
me.   Beside the joy of exercise I also have the pleasure of
being in the company of other people who are doing the same.
I think that if Eileen had still been alive she would have
enjoyed going there with me.

I have mentioned already those swims for Marie Curie,
through which I was able to raise £4-500 at a time.

If I am not engaged in these exercises, there are other
things I can do, such as taking walks and cycle rides. Exercise
has always been an important part of my life and it remains so.

If such variety of exercise is beyond you, then simply taking
a regular walk will do you a power of good. None of us at this
stage of life is preparing for the Olympics!

(3)   Spiritual responsibilities.

When you are left alone, then potentially you have more
time for church activities. I was already busy taking services in

other churches, and that did not change when I was left without Eileen. But there have been other responsibilities too and it may be the same for you.

I unexpectedly found myself chairing a little group of selectors, whose task it was to interview missionary candidates. This was a very fulfilling and worthwhile enterprise. After five years of this, I stepped down as chairman, but stayed on for one more year as a member of the committee. To some degree I kept up with the candidates afterwards, and, as I have said, even welcomed one to stay with me for a while when he had to come back from overseas to renew his visa. We had both worked for this mission for many years, but for me this was a new responsibility.

For many years I have been preaching regularly at the Belfast Chinese Church. Now I have been asked to serve as a trustee.

It may be that in your own church there will be posts to be filled for which you have both the ability and the time. It may be a question of service rather than leadership, but what does it matter if it is a response to God's call at this stage of our life?

(4)   Fresh Challenges

Life is not always predictable. Sometimes new opportunities appear before us which issue fresh challenges.

A new radio station opened on the peninsula. It was called Cuan FM. Although we were only on air for two weeks in the summer, it was a good opportunity to provide a service for the people who lived in this part of the world. I arranged a clergy rota for 'Thought for the Day', acted as disc jockey for Sunday morning hymns and even interviewed people, including a local MP, for our own 'Desert Island Discs'. It was good for me to be able to work with what for me was a new medium. Sadly, owing to lack of funding, the enterprise seems to be over. My moment of fame is over!

However, I am ready, if something else quite unexpected should also turn up, to give it a try.

(5)   Serving Others.

When we are no longer busy attending to the needs of a life partner, we have more time to be of service to other. This may be in simple ways, such as visiting sick and housebound friends; but there may also be something more.

Just when I thought my other duties were ending, I was asked to serve on the board of a new organization called Aimée's Hope, which was concerned to find a home for teenagers who had suffered difficult upbringings. At present this is at its early stages, with much still to be accomplished before it gets properly off the ground.. I trust that, by God's grace, this will become the means of rehabilitating many young people whose lives are in a mess.

It is exciting that, even in my late seventies, I can find new and worthwhile things to do. Life on earth is not over yet.

This is, of course, a list of activities which have been helpful for me. We are all different, and our own interests and skills may differ considerably. Some people like to give practical help with an aid agency, minister to young people on the streets in the early hours, help run a church canteen and so on. All I stress is that we should not be afraid to undertake anything new, for it enables us to move on.

Some people may like to serve as volunteers with a charitable organisation; some may like to meet up with people who share a common hobby, such as reading or singing; some may like to join a walking group; some may find their time taken up a lot with the needs of grandchildren. Our interests and our needs may vary; but it is worth pondering in what ways we can make our regular life more meaningful. Anything is better than a regular diet of daytime television!

Sixteen   Special Times

Whether we like it or not, there will be special days on which the absence of the one we loved is more keenly felt. It is because these days carry with them special memories.

(1)   Birthdays.

There seems to have been a revolution in the way birthdays are celebrated. For most of our lives we have enjoyed birthdays but without holding major celebrations. It was only when we turned 60 (and our birthdays were within three months of each other) that we had a special celebration and invited friends to go with us on a steam train and then to travel by boat up the River Dart. These days, however, for many people every birthday is a major affair, and when one's age carries a nought then it is a time for pulling out all the stops. .

On the occasion of Eileen's 70th birthday we celebrated in style by taking a short break in Prague, in the Czech Republic. On the day itself we took a cruise on the Voltava, where we ate the food provided and listened to some instrumentalists. They played jazz rather than Smetana, but that was not important. I felt so glad afterwards that we had created this special memory.

We would normally celebrate each other's birthday with cards and gifts and by going out for a meal at a restaurant. Such is the abundance of food served up in Irish restaurants that on one occasion our 'doggy bag' contained enough food for several further days of consumption! These were happy occasions which spoke of our love for each other. On my 65th, Eileen had invited various members of the family to make a special trip to Instow for a meal in a local hotel, and I never suspected a thing!

Now I often celebrate Eileen's birthday by going to visit my sons in London. As their wives' birthdays are roughly in the same time frame, we go out for a meal to celebrate the birthdays of all three women in our lives.

(2) Christmas.

Another such time is Christmas. Most years our sons would have come back to the family home to celebrate together; but occasionally we would go to stay with them in London. Our penultimate Christmas together we spent in Seoul with our son Andrew's wife's family.. There was quite a contrast between the traditional Korean cooking and the Christmas pudding which we produced afterwards. The last Christmas of Eileen's life we spent all together at our home in Ireland, but Eileen was unable to do her usual cooking and eating. The following year I went to London and we had Christmas dinner with an old friend of Eileen's at her new home. Subsequently we have followed the same routine of being together, but often it is just the males, and we now all share in the cooking. The main thing is that neither they nor I have to spend the festival alone. For those who live near their families, this is easier than it is for us. However, a flight between London and Belfast does not take long.

(3)   Wedding Anniversary.

Another special time is the wedding anniversary. Eileen and I would use this opportunity to go out for a meal. We had much to be thankful for, as God had given us such a happy marriage.

For me this memory is not so acute. Although I was good at remembering this day when Eileen was alive, I am happy to let this slip when I live alone. Some years I find the day passes without my even realizing it. In a sense, that is a mercy.

(4) Mother's Day.

The fourth Sunday in Lent is traditionally regarded as Mother's Day. At our church services, flowers are given to the women present. For my sons and myself, however, there is one very special woman no longer present in our lives, and it is not an easy day to get through. Fathers make up for this in June by having their own day. Although we hardly noticed this when Eileen was alive, I take great joy in being remembered now by my sons on that day. It means we have still preserved some sense of family.

(5) Anniversary of the Death

A further event is the remembrance of the death. I am usually acutely aware of that date when it comes up each year, but there is no major attempt to commemorate it. It is just a matter of getting on with life, having made proper adjustments. There is also scope for thanking God for all that was positive in the relationship while Eileen was still alive.

Now we are bound by time, and dates like these are important; but Eileen is, by contrast, beyond time, and I will be so one day.

Seventeen. Visible means of Support.

Some of us may feel we are perfectly capable of looking after our own newly-single lives without any outside support; but not all of us may feel capable of this.

(1) Regular Means.

If we are Christians, then we have the Lord's support. He is always there for us. Although we cannot talk to our spouse any more, we can talk to God, and we know that he hears us. He is just the same as he always was; in fact, he understands our current problems more than anyone. It is not the same as having someone's physical presence and a hand to press, but it is still a great help.

If we are Christians, then it is likely that we also belong to a church fellowship. Our fellow Christians are thus like a family to us. We know they are concerned about our welfare, and are ready to listen if we want to share anything. In some cases, especially when we are elderly and in poor health, we may receive Christian visitors, who will seek to encourage us.. Sometimes they may give practical support. There is one couple from church who have me round for a meal once a week even so many years after Eileen's death, and they are also available for practical help should there be a problem with the car or the house. Although for me the main emphasis has been on empathising with others, I recognise that for many it is a great boost to have friends from church (or elsewhere) who will show them that same empathy, which includes listening carefully to the outpouring of feelings. Others from church may encourage us by indicating new responsibilities which they think might be good for us – and for others – at this stage. It can be useful to belong to a small house group, where there is mutual love and acceptance. I also find that our mission, OMF International especially in its Irish context, has become like an extended family for me.

For many bereaved people the wider family is very important. They spend a lot of time with children and grandchildren, and there is a deep sense of belonging together. In my case, my two sons live a long way off in London, but we exchange visits from time to time. I have no grandchildren, so there is no bonding there; but I make an annual visit to Blackpool to see my birth family, that includes my great-niece, the one family member of that new generation. I am an exception, however, and most people in my situation would be able to spend a lot of time with children and grandchildren, and this makes the process of bereavement much easier to bear.

It is good also to have a wide circle of personal friends, whether Christian or not – people with whom we can exchange visits and with whom we can go on expeditions. There are others who may live too far from us for such get-togethers, but in these days of technology Skype, Facebook and Twitter can be useful means of regular contact, and smartphones can also serve a useful purpose.

We must be aware, however, that there are people who feel very uncomfortable in the presence of the bereaved. They suffer from embarrassment, and they do not know how to react. If we have friends like that, let us recall that it is their problem, not ours, and make allowances for this.

(2) Support Services.

For some people the sorrow of bereavement continues to be hard to bear. In such cases it is not wrong to seek help from counselling services. There are bereavement counsellors who know exactly what we are going through and are qualified to give us the support that we need to carry us through these anguished times. We are not afraid to go to the doctor with our medical emergencies; why, then, should we avoid seeking help from these people if our need is great? It does not mean that there is something wrong with our faith. They will not, of course, be able to bring our loved one back, but they will tap into resources that will help us to cope better.

(3) The Positive Side.

Not everything about bereavement is negative. Now we have plenty of time for personal outings, visiting others, reading, watching television and for pursuing our hobbies. Much of this this will be for pleasure; but there are occasions when a book may speak clearly to us in our difficult times and give us courage. The same may be said for certain television programmes.

If we want to make a journey, we are free to 'get up and go' without having to consider the needs of someone else. It is also cheaper to travel alone! Now and again we may come upon a hotel that does not charge a single supplement!

If we were living on a desert island, then coping with our newly single life might be difficult, but all around us there are others who are only too willing to help us in this time of adjustment. It would be foolish then to hide away from others and to try to deal with our emotions unaided. Even so, it primarily to God that we turn as Christians, knowing that, since we belong to him, we are not alone.

Eighteen   Older – and Wiser?

For Eileen the process of ageing is over. Now she has a new ageless existence in heaven. For me, however, the process of ageing continues. I am largely blessed with good health and I often thank God for this. In fact, people often express surprise when they hear how old I really am.

(1) My Own Limitations.

Even I, however, have my limits. There came a day, as have said, when the doctor told me that, because of wear and tear on the knees, I must no longer jog. This came as a big blow, almost like an extra bereavement. Something that had been a large part of my life was now missing.

Maybe, I thought, I could jog a little. I tried it, and had a searing pain in the thigh; and when I took painkillers this made me vomit. In all this, I was all too conscious of my human frailty.

Whether I like it or not, I am ageing all the time. My sight and my hearing are not quite what they used to be. Some arthritis is getting into my hands. No doubt there will be other limitations which, in time, I shall be obliged to accept. It helps, however, to be grateful for what we can still do, and worrying about an uncertain future is somewhat pointless.

There are others, though who, on reaching my age, have severe physical limitations. Some would have spouse and other family members around them, so that there is no need to suffer alone. If I were to become unwell, though, there is nobody at hand on whom I could rely without bringing my own sons on a long journey. However, there is little point in worrying about this. If my health should decline, God can handle the problem.

(2) My Own Advantages.

There are men in the Bible who really prospered in old age. One of them is Caleb, who, even when claiming his long awaited inheritance, was not afraid to risk some conflict to get it. I think too of old Simeon, who knew he could die happily since he had lived to see the promised Messiah.

Recently I met with other local clergy and we prayed for one another. I heard myself described as an 'elder statesman'. I sensed that, despite my age, I still had some value in the local community, and this felt good. We are the fruit of what our years have made us, and this includes much that is positive. If we lived in China, we would be much respected for our seniority.

(3) An Undetermined End.

One day I joined other members of Eileen's family to celebrate the 80th birthday of her cousin Mildred. It seemed odd that Eileen was not there herself to celebrate the occasion. I could not help wondering what would happen to me on my eightieth birthday – assuming that I would have one!

Nobody can determine the length of his or her life. That is beyond our control. In fact, it would be rather scary if we knew the day we were going to leave this earth. All we know is that people are living longer than they used to do. The period of living alone could be quite a long one. It has been suggested that 1 in 5 of those living now will reach the age of 100. But the actual time of our going is for God to determine.

Whether long or short, however, that is as nothing when compared with eternity. We are not simply living for this world, as many are. Let us determine to spend our time well, but to do so in the light of what is still to come when the Lord promotes us. Let us pray also that when our homecall comes we shall be ready for it.

Nineteen.   In Loving Memory.

Sometimes it comforts me to see how Eileen's influence lives on even after her death. Two months after her passing I visited the local primary school, where a rhododendron bush had been planted in her memory; for so many of the young mothers appreciated the relaxation classes which she had held there. The accompanying plaque spoke of how much she had been appreciated.

A plaque was also erected in the new community garden, for much of the inspiration for creating this garden had come from Eileen. It pleases me now to see how the garden is thriving. Much better than that old barren field with a horse grazing, though the horse may have other ideas!

Shortly before Eileen's illness, we visited the Bishop to voice our concern for the churches of the peninsula. Even before her death changes began: clergy from various denominations had begun to meet regularly for prayer and fellowship and praise services were beginning to be held twice a year to bring together people from various churches. When over 200 people crowded into Christ Church, Carrowdore, for such a celebration recently, the Bishop commented on the results of her vision. These features continue up to the present day. Yes, Eileen has left her mark on this area.

But she has also left her mark on our own lives. Every year, as near to her birth date of August 7 as possible, I meet up with my two sons and their spouses to share a meal together in her memory. This has become for us a valued institution, and it affords us the scope to remember together how much we owe to her.

There are memorials in sound and vision that we can turn to at any time. One of these is the video of our wedding, which was such a memorable occasion. There is also a video of Eileen's mother's 80th birthday, in which Eileen can also be seen. In addition I have a brief video in which Eileen speaks on BBC Newsline of how God healed her after she had a cancerous melanoma. Her desire to exalt Christ on that occasion comes over very clearly. I do not make a habit of watching these, but it is good to know that they are there.

Sometimes, as well as reading Eileen's poems and her limited journals, I come across a passage in a book she has underlined and which has something to say to me. One such passage, in a devotional book, read, "Our present, with fears within and foes without, may all be put into His strong hand so that both we and our circumstances are held and controlled by Him Who is holy and loving and wise." So such truths become important not just for Eileen but also for me.

I like to think also that I as a person was greatly changed for the better by knowing Eileen, and so that too is an ongoing reminder of all that she meant to me. Meeting Eileen and uniting my life with hers are the greatest things that ever happened to me. Whilst I am alive, her influence lives on in me.

In any good marriage there should be a similar effect. Each of us is the fruit of a very special relationship.

20. Drawing Alongside

This book is mainly addressed to the person who has suffered bereavement. It may be however, that you have not yourself suffered bereavement, but are anxious to help someone in that condition. Some reference has been made to this in earlier chapters. This final chapter simply provides a few hints to help you in that task. These thoughts are not taken from some textbook but simply from my own experience of human relationships.

(1) Be natural.

In relating to the newly bereaved it does not help to communicate in hushed whispers or to studiously avoid mentioning the deceased. Be natural. Be yourself. Be the same as you were before. The bereaved person has enough to deal with in accepting the loss of that loved one, and if it also entails a loss of other natural relationships it will hinder rather than help them on the road to recovery.

(2) Be a good listener.

Our primary purpose is not to give advice and instruction to our deceased friend. It is rather to be a sounding board when they want to speak of their feelings. Everyone who is going through a time of stress needs to have good listeners. Often good listening can be more helpful than speaking. Give that person your full attention. Don't look as if you are in a hurry to get away. This is of far greater value than trite suggestions as to how to cope.

(3)   Offer hospitality.

I have already mentioned the friends who have given me a weekly meal since Eileen's loss. Although I am perfectly capable of cooking my own food, it is good to experience the love that accompanies this provision. I do not have to eat alone every time. Maybe we can offer a place at our own table to people who are experiencing a new singleness.

(4) Pray for them.

We may not understand all they are going through; we may not understand all the problems they face and all the changes they must make, but we can pray. When a friend is newly bereaved, I often put that person on my daily prayer list for a while, asking God to help them in a time of difficult adjustments. It may help them too if they know that others are praying.

The author, Shelden Vanauken, writing about the loss of his wife Davy, testifies to the help which his friendship with C. S. Lewis gave him. This was not long before Lewis had to suffer his own encounter with such loss.

In all these things we are showing that we care for our grieving friends by behaving in such natural and loving ways. However they are coping with their new life, it is good for them to know that they are not alone but have caring friends.

Epilogue   Surreal.

On the anniversary of the death of C. S. Lewis I was invited to preach in the Belfast church where he had been baptised. There I met a Stormont representative called Sammy Douglas, who invited me to attend a function at that seat of government two days later when portraits of Lewis and of the poet Seamus Heaney would be unveiled. I decided it might be an interesting event to attend, so I duly turned up. What followed took me completely by surprise.

Just before the ceremony was due to begin, I was informed that I would personally be unveiling the Lewis portrait. There were a few introductory speeches. In one of them, Mr. Douglas referred to something I had said in my Sunday sermon, when I described how, no longer able to read properly because of her illness, Eileen was content to listen on headphones to the Narnia stories and received some comfort from those.

After the ceremony the First Minister and the Deputy First Minister came up to shake hands. We then stood there with Mrs Heaney and a few others to face a barrage of popping cameras.

Over the meal that followed, when I was no longer in the limelight, I was talking with a fellow widower who professed to be an atheist, and who found his single life very lonely. I was able to tell him how my faith had helped me over these difficult years. In a way, that was more valuable than simply unveiling a painting.

This was just one of the unexpected and surreal experiences that have happened to me since my bereavement; but such events serve to encourage me and enable me to feel there is plenty still for me to experience before I also leave this world.

SOME USEFUL BOOKS

"Beyond the Exit Door" - Robert J. Vetter

"Living Through Grief" - Harold Bayman

"Good Grief" - Granger E. Westberg

"Tracing the Rainbow" - Pablo Martinez and Ali Hull

"Living With Bereavement" - Sue Mayfield

"Pathways to Joy" - Eileen Mitford

"More" - Simon Ponsonby.

"A Severe Mercy" - Sheldon Vanauken.

"A Grief Observed" - C. S. Lewis.

44033932R00067

Printed in Poland
by Amazon Fulfillment
Poland Sp. z o.o., Wrocław